MY DEAR LOVING SISTERS

Tea and Stories from an Audacious Life

By Fatoun Ali

CONTENTS

A Note from the Author

A Note from the Author

My Dear Sister, my purpose for writing this book is to empower *you*. In doing so, I will be talking about my personal life--how I empowered *myself* when no one else would. I know that some readers may wonder if I am betraying my family or my community by telling my stories of pain, neglect, and ultimate triumph, so that you may perhaps create a new and satisfying story for your life as well.

Some of you will shame me for sharing stories from my life. Others may judge me because they don't want to hear the truth. But many women will thank me for sharing the raw truth about my life at a moment when they may not yet have the courage to tell *their* truth. The truth can be painful, but it will set you free to make the necessary changes in your own life.

The fact is that I want to inspire change. I want to inspire change in my community, in my world, and in my environment. I want to help women, mothers, daughters, and grandmothers, anyone who made any mistakes in their lives. The only way that can happen is to tell the truth.

I also want to change the way our *men* treat us, and the attitude held by many men and women in our culture that *women's lives are less important than men's lives.* This attitude often starts in our homes when, as children, girls are expected and taught to do all the housework and chores, including caring for younger siblings, while boys are given freedom and privileges. In order to change men's attitudes and behavior, we have to teach them to respect girls and women while they are young. And *we* have to respect our daughters and other women.

I want things to change for the better. If we recognize our mistakes but keep them hidden (which a lot of us do), we keep our pain. We want to be seen as successful and loving. We want to project a good image of our families.

But the truth is, I come from a very dysfunctional family. Some of my experiences will be sadly familiar to readers of this book. For those fortunate enough to have come from a healthy, happy family, I hope you have empathy and understanding for people who have been through family strife and dysfunction, especially those with even more difficult and damaging families than mine.

If we don't change our dysfunctional families, if we don't acknowledge the problem and the pain it causes and put a stop to it, our misery and struggle will carry on for generation after generation.

I want that pain to stop here with me, with my offspring. That's why I am sharing my personal experiences in this guide. The very first step in change is acknowledging the truth.

I know—because I have experienced it—that you can heal your body, mind, and soul through storytelling! You can't heal if you don't know what you are healing from.

This is my story.

Introduction

My Dear Loving Sisters ~

I came to the United States alone in 1998. I was 8 months pregnant with my second child. My husband wouldn't arrive in America for two more months. I arrived voiceless—literally, I could not speak English. I had lost my firstborn child to muscular dystrophy, and I didn't know if my second child would survive. I found myself in San Diego, California with a husband and no money, no job, no car, no education (I couldn't even write my own name), and no documentation. I didn't know who I was, where I was, or how anything was ever going to get better. I only knew I had *faith in God* and that I would eventually, somehow, be okay.

This move to the U.S. saved my life. I would've surely died in the Somali refugee camp after over a decade living in uncertainty, extreme poverty, and worse. The fact that I made it out to a fresh start in a new country gave me hope for my life and proved that my faith in God and myself were well-placed. Today, my life looks even better than the one I dared to imagine for myself. I am thriving as a mother to my four children. I am a business owner, coach, and mentor to so many other women. I give to my community. I have made a name for myself. What I dreamed of was possible!

If your story is like my story, you've come through a *lot*. You've moved to a new country. You didn't speak the language when you first arrived. You have family to take care of. It's a different climate, you have to get used to different weather. The closest person in your life (your husband or another family member) might even be abusive to you—emotionally, mentally, financially, physically, and psychologically. None of this is okay. It wasn't okay for me, and it's *not* okay for you, either. You're lost, confused, lonely, afraid, and *overwhelmed.* You doubt yourself, your worth. You are drained—the strength you need to survive (and help your family survive!) is a dim and distant memory. How do you even begin to put yourself together in this state?

My Dear Loving Sister, *no*. You are not done. There is so much more for you in this life. You *are strong enough.* You are valuable beyond measure. You have gifts and energy you never knew were part of you. Allah has a different path for you than misery and fear. And if you've picked up this book (no matter where you come from, your faith, or your skin color), you are ready to discover that path and begin to walk it with me.

The purpose of this book is to uplift you, to empower you, to encourage you, and to help you identify and find the resources you need to *thrive* in this life and after. (I say "after" since, in my Muslim faith and many other religions and spiritual paths, there is a belief that the good deeds that you do in this world will benefit you when you die.)

I want to show you how, when you are exhausted and fed up about the difficulties in life, to not give up. To not get stuck. To move forward and find your peace and purpose. And find resources and friends and mentors who can help you and guide you to a place of strength and abundance you perhaps never even knew existed before now.

In this guide, I'll share stories from my life. Lessons that I've learned. Life hacks, tips, and practical insights that will save you time and energy. I'll ask questions designed to help you clarify your goals and take positive action.

I was born in Somalia. Civil war broke out in my country when I was thirteen and I left my country as a teenager. I had no money, no education (not even grade school!), and didn't speak English. I have experienced exhausting poverty, physical and emotional abuse, betrayal in both love and business. And —I lost two of my precious children as babies.

Despite these extreme hardships and challenges, I have been able to slowly but steadily build a meaningful, secure, and joyful new life for myself and my family in the United States. With the help of two kind women, I escaped from an abusive living situation. I got a job and went to night school to learn English. I made friends and found mentors and people I could trust and new opportunities. I've learned a lot along the way. I want to share what I've learned with you.

I call you my Sisters because in my Islamic faith, we're all one family, brothers and sisters. I used the phrase "tea and stories" in the subtitle of this book because in Somalia, elders would gather under the welcoming shade of a large tree to hold discussions on important matters, as together they made significant decisions that changed lives. People, especially women, would meet under a tree in the afternoon for fun and community. Sharing tea and stories *(shaah iyo sheeko)* was part of these gatherings.

My goal for this book is that women of all backgrounds, all religions, and all colors see this as a guide for them–with a special tenderness for my immigrant Somali Sisters.

And that, regardless of your background, education, religious beliefs, you know—you remember!—that you are powerful, you are here for a purpose, you are amazing, and that Allah created you whole and complete.

How to use this book

You'll see as you read that each chapter is divided into sections:

- **Stories from my life,** so that you know I've experienced what you have experienced, or what you're still going through now, or you want to feel empowered in your own life. It's so helpful to know we're not alone in the struggle!
- **Tips and suggestions** for how to make changes in your life–so that not only *you* live a life of satisfaction, love, and joy, but that our whole culture begins to change because of the *work you do for yourself.*
- **Questions for reflection and action** at the end of each chapter, so you can pinpoint where you most want to begin in your life today with the transformation you seek.

Read each chapter and digest the stories and tips. Take a moment to reflect on your own journey and how it is the same or different from mine. Then, answer the questions at the end of each chapter and look for the areas where change could be possible in your life. Keep coming back to this book often—as if we are friends sharing tea together. *There will always be a story for you and a helpful suggestion in these pages when you are sad, angry, lonely, exhausted, or overwhelmed.*

It's best to take tiny steps as you work for bigger transformation. You'll notice that my growth and development happened over many years. It took me a long time to get out of the devastating situations I was in early in life. After over two decades of healing and support and miracles, I am finally thriving today. And, *I'm still a work in progress*—I'm still growing and learning every single day.

Your success isn't about how fast the journey goes, but that you've agreed to be on it in the first place. Together, we can move mountains for ourselves and others when we agree to move forward–even when it seems impossible. *If you can learn to imagine the life you want for yourself, you can have it,* Dear Sister.

May this book be the first (or 100th!) of the many steps that will lead you to a thriving, satisfying life you love.

–In warmth, tenderness, and kindness,

Fatoun Ali

PART 1:
CULTIVATE A HEALTHY LOVING RELATIONSHIP WITH YOURSELF

Chapter 1
Listen to Your Inner Voice

The first time I listened to my inner voice, it saved my life.

I was four years old, walking around my grandparents' fruit and vegetable farm. I fell asleep in the middle of the day. It was really hot and I fell asleep on the sand outside. And when I woke up, it was because something told me to wake up.

Something told me, *"Wake up!"* Someone was tapping me on my shoulder. When I opened my eyes, I was lost and scattered. I didn't know where I was. I tried to get up and I couldn't get up.

I had fallen asleep on my right side. My right cheek, my hip, were deep in the sand. I had sand sticking to my skin. My skin was sweaty, wet with little bumps everywhere because of the sand marks. My left side was burned because of the hot sun. Dry, burned, hot.

I was numb. I was dehydrated. I couldn't move. My limbs were too weak to walk. So I had to crawl. I crawled all the way to the kitchen. Nobody knew where I was, a four-year-old! Nobody looked for me.

But there *was* someone looking out for me. A voice, my inner guidance. I heard the voice telling me, *"Get up!"* And I listened to that voice.

I couldn't walk. So I crawled and I crawled. I crawled to the kitchen. I found the shade.

I was thirsty and my throat was dry. I found a cup. I filled it with water and I drank it. I found a piece of *injera*, which we call sourdough bread. It is tradition in Somali culture to eat injera in the morning. I grabbed that; I ate it. I ate that piece of injera bread. And I drank that water. I stayed in the shade until my skin cooled down.

The voice? That was *my* voice. That was the first time I heard—and listened to—my inner voice, telling me to stand up, to move. *To get up and not to give up.*

From that day, I knew I was alone in this world because my parents were not there. My mom was not there emotionally and physically for me until I was seven years old; my dad was not there at all. I was only four years old.

It was hard. I remember that. But I had my inner voice, my inner knowing. That was my awakening call.

You have this inner voice, this inner knowing inside of you, too. Can you hear it calling to you? What does it say? Is it so distant and quiet that you can't make out the words? My Dear Sister, *start listening again. That voice will never fail you, even when everything outside of you does.*

Always, *always* listen to your gut instinct. By doing so, you will find inner peace, your core, and your strength. It is an essential skill that will help you in literally every situation in your life. It is an *always accessible* source of wisdom and guidance.

Whatever you're going through, know that whatever is happening, it's not *you*. It's not who you are. It's just you *going through this experience*.

For me, no matter what I was going through—family strife, civil war, even facing time in jail for *not* listening to my inner voice and trusting the wrong people in a business setting—I knew that there was a light at the end of the tunnel. I knew that whatever I was going through at that moment, it was just a transition.

It was hard. But *something* was telling me everything was going to be okay. My inner voice. You can get through this hard time and the ones ahead and you have to listen to that voice. Sometimes it's hard. Sometimes we block it.

If you really pay close attention, your inner voice will guide you—if you let it. And listening to that voice, listening to that feeling, it will tell you if something's wrong. Like if your husband or one of your children is not telling you the truth, you know. You can feel it. But we ignore that and give people who lie the benefit of the doubt.

Starting to pay attention to your body's wisdom, your inner voice, is the beginning of empowering yourself. It's the beginning of respecting yourself. It's part of the process of growth. Of getting stronger.

Learning to pay attention to your feelings and your gut instincts can be scary and uncomfortable at first. It can be scary because you may be doubting yourself also, wondering:

Is this true?
Am I just imagining this?
Am I misinterpreting this?

There's a lot of self-doubt when you first listen within yourself, but it gets easier and easier the more you believe in yourself. The more you hear the words. The more you ask questions.

After so many years of listening to my inner voice, I never ignore it now. And always, always if I know there's something wrong, or if someone is not being honest with me, I try to ask that person to tell me the truth. You know, *"Are you telling me what's really happening? Just the way it is. We can fix things. We can communicate. We can heal from it."*

Then the truth comes out. Then I know my inner voice is telling me the truth.

How to tune into and trust your inner voice

- Find a quiet moment to yourself (even if it's in the car or bedroom with the door closed!)
- Take at least 5 deep breaths, all the way into your belly.
- Tell yourself that in this moment, you are safe, you are okay. It is safe for your inner voice to start speaking to you.
- Allow any mundane or worrisome thoughts to float through your mind without paying too much attention to them.
- Gently listen deeper within yourself. Notice any thoughts or words that seem like they are coming from within you, but might feel also like a kind and supportive voice that's not exactly yours—like it's coming from a "higher" or "bigger" place. What does that voice want you to know today?
- Write down the words or thoughts you "heard" in a notebook or journal.
- Find a moment each day to repeat this exercise.

Questions to help you learn to listen to and trust your inner wisdom as you move forward in your own life:

- When your inner voice speaks to you, how do you respond?

  ____

  ____

  ____

  ____

- Ask yourself, *"Where is this uneasy feeling coming from? Is it coming from work colleagues? My husband? My friends? Or somewhere within me?"*

- Ask yourself, *"What is this feeling guiding me away from? Is it guiding me away from danger, pain, setbacks, and sorrow? Is it guiding me toward truth, safety, personal growth, and happiness?"*

~~~
~~~

My Dear Sisters, the most important thing you can do for your life is to become best friends with yourself. Listen deeply to your inner voice. When it speaks to you, please sit with it and listen to it carefully. Your inner voice can truly save you and protect you. *It is the only place to begin healing your life.*

Chapter 2

Listen to Your Guardian Angels

Throughout my life, I've been guided by angels.

I believe, and my Muslim faith teaches, that we each have guiding angels throughout our life. We have angels on our right shoulder and our left shoulder that always guide us and always record our deeds, whether good or bad.

I consulted an imam (a Muslim religious leader), and he referred me to the Quran verse that includes the phrase, "*For each one there are successive angels before and behind, protecting them by Allah's command. Indeed, Allah would never change a people's state of favor until they change their own state of faith.*"

When I listen to my angels, they help me get through some of the darkest and most difficult times of my life. My angel guidance discernment is so strong now that when my angels are offering me guidance, I feel like somebody's tapping on my shoulders. Or whispering in my ears, telling me to get out of this situation or to not get into that situation. In that way, it's different from my inner voice guidance.

My angels have nothing to do with my own feelings. It's like someone guiding me—angels, guiding angels, sent by Allah and telling me what I need to do. Their voices are so strong, it's like someone is talking to me out loud.

Here's an example of a time when I heard my guiding angels' voices, but didn't listen to them. I paid a very steep price for that; a price that impacted my life for years.

I was working with financial partners who turned out to be dishonest and my business was failing, I *knew* something was wrong. But I felt paralyzed —like I was suffocating, like I had tape over my mouth. I couldn't say or do anything about it. I ignored the feeling–the voice. I convinced myself my guides were wrong.

I was not only aware of the feeling, I knew I was being pushed to act. My angels wanted me to do something about the situation. I heard their message to me, but it was a message that I couldn't handle and didn't know how to handle.

I had worked so hard to set up my business, a business I truly believed in and knew was needed—a home health agency specializing in Somali clients and staff. I had initially trusted my business partners, both men, and thought they knew more about the financial aspects of the business than I did. That turned out to be a very costly mistake.

We had a verbal agreement rather than a written contract, because the business was in my name. That was another big mistake.

Their "help" turned into basically a shakedown. The men had deep connections in the Minneapolis Somali community because they had been in Minnesota for a long time. They were businessmen. They were respected. They told me that no one would do business with my agency unless they were part of the business. (I am from a minority tribe in Somalia and there is still a lot of discrimination against certain tribes within the U.S. Somali communities.)

But the men told me they didn't care about my tribe. They said, *"We're here to do business. And because we're with you, we can get clients for you."*

They gave me what turned out to be fraudulent financial advice. I ended up being held liable for fraud, while they both escaped any consequence. There was nothing legally linking them to my business, nothing in writing, just my word against theirs. They changed their phone numbers and disappeared.

I ended up spending time in jail. I was ordered to pay restitution. I was three months pregnant with my fifth child and suffering debilitating morning sickness, made worse by the poor jail diet and my concern for my older two children, who were being cared for by a friend.
I was heartsick and angry that my trust in my business partners had resulted in my life being disastrously derailed in so many ways.

I had ignored the guidance of my angels, and I was paying a steep price.

Once I finished my jail time, I still had to pay restitution. Because I didn't have money to pay it in full, I had to make a monthly payment on top of all my other bills. It took me a long time to pay off this debt. On top of everything else, I now had a felony conviction on my record that made it nearly impossible for me to get hired for any job.

Every single job I applied for, I was denied employment because of something that I didn't do. I didn't know how I was going to be able to make a living or pay my bills.

Working as an interpreter saved me. Becoming self-employed was my only option for income. When you're self-employed, you don't have to go through any background checks that most employers require.

Being an immigrant (a part of my identity that held me back in so many ways in America) actually became my superpower in this situation. *If I didn't speak Somali, if I weren't bilingual, I could have been homeless.* I could have been on the streets. I couldn't do anything.

The felony conviction also impacted my path to getting U.S. citizenship. It meant I had to wait for many years to apply for citizenship. And it made it very risky for me to travel outside the United States, as I didn't have a U.S. passport. I could have done so with travel documents or by getting a Somali passport but, as a mother, I didn't want to take the chance that I couldn't return to my country. Twelve years later, I am *still* working on becoming a U.S. citizen.

As women, we tend to trust others because we are taught not to believe in ourselves. We are taught not to trust ourselves. We often put men in a higher position than ourselves. It was a lesson that taught me this lesson: *My life is more important than a business partner.* And *your* life is more important than a business partner. If I had listened to my angels, I would have been spared a lot of pain.

So know that, regardless of what's happening in your life, you are not alone. You are never alone. Allah (God) and his guardian angels are with you, my Dear Sister.There are angels, higher powers looking out for you. And that if you learn to listen to them and follow their guidance, the angels will watch over you and touch your life and save you.

In our religion, we don't believe in having pictures of guardian angels or God or Muhammad or prophets. We believe in higher powers and the unseen. We don't see them, but they're there guiding us. No matter what—even if you are homeless, even if you're in jail, even if you have lost everything—you still have a guardian angel. Angel guidance is free. It doesn't cost anything. All you have to do to get it is listen and trust.

Guardian angels, like our inner voice, are a source of strength and guidance that is *always* available to us, in any circumstance.

How to find and listen to your Guardian Angels

Similar to the tips you read about listening to your Inner Voice, here are some ways to start trusting and listening to your Guardian Angels:

- When you wake up in the morning—even before you get out of bed—breathe deeply and ask your Guardian Angels what message or guidance they have for your day.
- When you feel your own thoughts creep in about fear or anxiety or even what you might have for breakfast, let yourself sink deeper than your thoughts for a moment.
- At first, you may hear nothing. It may take several mornings before you can tune into your Guardian Angels, but they are near.
- Begin to notice in your body how you feel after you ask the question to your Angels. Sometimes you might get a signal in your gut or your chest or your throat that tells you what direction to go when you have a choice to make or something hard to get through.
- When you turn toward those body sensations, notice if you get a message or guidance that seems as though it's beyond just you.
- Listen deeply to those words and see if they make sense to you. Trust the words and the truth of the message, even if you don't act on the guidance right away.

Questions to help you learn to listen to and trust your guardian angels as you move forward in your own life:

- Do you believe in guardian angels and divine guidance?

____

____

____

____

____

____

- Are you open to receiving messages and guidance from your angels? Why or why not?

- Have you ever felt you were getting messages from your angels or guides and didn't know what to do? How did you respond?

- If you followed your angel's guidance, what was the outcome?

- If you did not follow your angel's guidance, what was the outcome?

____

____

____

~~~

My Blessed Sisters, my message to you is to believe in yourself and your ability to listen to your higher powers. It is crucial for us to pay close attention to our feelings and our guardian angels. Having faith in Allah and his guardian angels can serve us in powerful ways.
~~~

Chapter 3

Create Time for Yourself Every Day

Every day, no matter what else I do, I take time to do a little work on myself.

One of the most important ways to start to change your life is to reclaim some time just for yourself, every single day. It can be as simple as sitting with your thoughts, something a lot of women, especially East African women, *don't* do.

It is very difficult to take this time, especially if you are a single mother with many responsibilities, but also because of where we came from in our culture. For women, it's all about caring for other people.

When we have children, we're always caring for them. When we have a husband, we care for our husband. We care for our in-laws, our parents, our cousins and family, but it's really very hard to think about ourselves. Self-care is not something that is encouraged or taught for women in our culture or our background.

My experience as a Somali woman is that we don't know how to sit with our feelings. With our thoughts. We pray five times a day, but we do it quickly and resume our running around. It's really easy for our lives to be all about running around and doing things—in the community, taking care of children, taking care of the household, taking care of family members, taking care of our husband, working, working, working and then crashing at night, exhausted.

At the end of a long day of caring for everyone else, we don't even get ten to fifteen minutes to ourselves! Everyone else's needs come first, and then we have nothing left for ourselves. We don't take even a few minutes for ourselves each day to sit with our thoughts, to sit with our emotions, and evaluate what's happening in our lives and around us.

I created a yoga class for women in my community in which participants would lie down, relax, and do deep breathing. But my students got bored, telling me things like: *"This is not exercise"* and *"This is not helping us, it's so boring, we need to be doing something..."*

I told them that to reconnect with your soul, you have to reclaim some time for yourself. You must relax your mind and relax your body. It's like sleep; it restores your body, your mind, and your spirit. The simple daily practice of taking some time alone with and for yourself will help your spiritual life, it will help your emotional life, it will help your physical life! You'll have more energy and more focus.

In most East African cultures, the importance of self-care for women—settling in, being grounded, relaxing and taking a deep breath—is not recognized in our community, by men or women. Our culture teaches us that it's selfish for a woman to take any time for herself.

But it's not selfish, even from a caregiving perspective! Because if you don't take care of yourself, how can you take care of anyone else? It's impossible to care sustainably for others when we are so tired and empty that we have nothing to give. We turn into robots when we do this.

So, not only African women, *every* woman deserves to take care of herself. Every woman deserves to take time for herself to nurture her soul and body and mind so she can be the best woman she can be. Then, she can show up for herself first, and then for her family, her children, her husband, her community, her friends, and her colleagues.

Taking time for yourself also makes possible a true spiritual connection with God. Praying and running around and doing no more than the minimum mandatory requirement is not enough! You have to connect with your soul. You have to connect with God by taking time for yourself. In order for your prayers to be accepted, you have to pray from your heart, from your mind, your soul, your body. You have to pay full attention, focus one hundred percent. It's necessary to stop "doing" and sit in some amount of stillness for this focus to happen and for God to find you and you to find God.

In a recent Google search, I found a Hadith quote that emphasizes this very point:

"When the servant comes close to Me (Allah) as far as a span of hand, I come to him as far as a forearm. When he comes to Me as far as a forearm, I come to him as far as the span of the outspread arms. When he comes to me walking, I come to him rushing."

–The Hadith

We pray five times a day and a lot of people pray just to pray. They do it quickly; they don't even think about it, but it's supposed to be a meditation for us. You connect with higher powers, you connect with God. You give all your problems and all your issues to God and that's why you're doing the morning prayer, afternoon prayer, late afternoon, evening, and at night.

Even if you cannot find another time, those five prayer times are an opportunity to take time for yourself and take an extra five minutes for each prayer.

Every year, I look back over the past twelve months to evaluate—and celebrate!—my progress. I ask myself: "*What did I do that improved my life? What did I accomplish? And what have I not yet accomplished that I still want to do?*"

Because every year my goal is to better myself—to improve myself, to gain something, to learn something new. I got an associate degree, then I got my bachelor's degree. I repaired my credit, I bought a home, I started a business, I started a nonprofit, I built a healthy relationship… I learned the Holy Quran and learned how to read and write my own Somali language.

I want there to always be something new and worthwhile that I've done: giving back to the community, contributing to a charitable organization, mentoring more girls, or even just something new that I'm excited about. Something so I can feel great. So, I can say, "*Honestly, I did that. I accomplished that with Allah's help*".

If you want to learn a new language, write a book, improve your heart, or whatever it is you want, you are adding value to your life. This added value can uplift you and encourage you and keep you motivated. When you do something new and exciting, you stay active and young because every time you do something good, you feel good. You're improving your life, you're improving yourself.

I have this ideal of practicing self-love. For me, coming to the U.S. and learning about the culture, getting an education, and being a single parent, I discovered that in order to survive and have emotional stability and mental clarity, I had to be really creative to come up with time for myself every day.

I'm a morning person, so for me it was easier and more productive to get up early. (At 4:00 a.m. or 5:00 a.m.) Before my children wake up, I take time for myself, whether I exercise, read, write or just meditate.

If you are an afternoon person, you can take time during your lunch hour instead to sit with your thoughts, meditate, or do some walking. If you're a night owl, you can give yourself some self-care time in the evening when you put the children down to sleep. You can sit with your thoughts and evaluate your life.

Another thing that's important for self-care: Find or create a space that is just for you. One option is to create a space in your bedroom. For example, I have a little area next to my bed that is just for me. There, I relax, I meditate, I pray.

I am very fortunate to have a bigger space to live in now than I did in the past, when I had to use my car or my bed as my meditation, self-reflection, and goal-setting spot. So, in my home, I have also created a relaxing area in our four-season sunroom. I've designated a whole area for relaxation for me and/or my children. I have my books, I have my mat to pray on. I have a couple of comfortable chairs in that area as we go there to meditate and pray.

Take time to yourself, go sit down, relax, close your eyes, and just let go of everything you have to do for five minutes. This action may feel impossible, awkward, or even anxious at first. But your tasks will still be there after you're done meditating. Everyone will be okay without you for a short while. You will feel more energized and nourished afterward. It's very important to well-being for yourself as a mother, as a woman, or anyone, really. And teaching your children the importance of self-care by example is good parenting. It will help them be better parents and adults in the future when they value themselves enough to take the same time for themselves as they do for others.

If you can take even twenty or thirty minutes for yourself each day, this simple practice will improve your life in so many ways. In addition to feeling grounded and having more energy and focus, you'll be creating space and time to be able to start to dream, set goals, and make plans for your life. It is a gift that you give to yourself that will help you and everyone else in your life.

How to meditate

- Start small with 5 minutes of stillness. As you become more comfortable and regular with this time, add to it each week or month in 5 minute chunks. Set a timer if it helps you.
- Begin by breathing deeply for several breaths.
- Notice your thoughts—where do they naturally go?
- When you notice your thoughts straying toward everything you must do or thoughts of worry or fear, gently and kindly move your thoughts back to your body or your breath.
- Notice your body–how do you feel as you sit still? It's enough to simply notice how your gut feels, your chest, your throat. You might become aware of body parts that feel tired or sore. Send love and calm to those parts of you. This is you "healing" yourself.
- Let go of expecting anything "big" to happen. It is enough to connect with yourself for a short time.
- Know that meditation is a practice—you may not notice results for a while, or you may notice a greater sense of peace and calm right away. Everyone is different and no experience is wrong.

Questions to help you create time every day for yourself, for reflection, and for your dreams:

- What time of day would work best for you to take 15—30 minutes for yourself? (If you truly can't take 15—30 minutes for yourself each day, can you take an extra three, five or ten more minutes after each prayer to calm your mind and connect with your soul?)

____

____

____

____

____

____

____

____

- What quiet corner or spot in your home could be your special relaxing space?

- What self-care action (sitting with thoughts, reading, meditation, stretching, etc.) would feel best for you at this time in your life?

- Do you do any exercise such as walking, dancing, swimming, or weightlifting to stay healthy and fit?

~~~

My Beloved Sisters, my hope is that you think of self-care as recharging your soul, being whole so you can take better care of yourself and your loved ones. I know that when you are well-rested and make self-care a daily practice, you will have more energy, more hope, and more joy in your own life and more positive energy to share with others.
~~~

Chapter 4

Set Goals to Prioritize and Manage Your Time

I didn't know anything about goal setting, time management, or financial planning until I came to Minnesota. When we don't set goals, manage our time, and financially plan our futures, we stay in our current and often hard situations. Nothing changes without vision, planning, and action.

In the last three chapters, we've covered how to listen to your Inner Voice, your Guardian Angels, and how to create time for yourself, even when there seems to be none available. Now, it's time to go to the next level.

When I got to Minnesota, I registered at Community Action (a local organization) for a program called Self-Sufficiency for Low-Income Families. It was a two-year program. And if you wanted to become successful, if you wanted to change yourself and achieve your goals, you had to complete the whole two years.

I remember wanting to change my life because I was in a new city and state. So I signed up. I had two children and I was trying to change my whole situation because I had just gone through a divorce, left a horribly abusive home, and moved all the way across the country..

I wanted to start fresh. When I came to Community Action in Minnesota and my family caseworker explained the program, I said, *"I'm in."*

That's where I learned time management. I learned how to set different goals for my life and for my family. I learned how to organize my life, my time, my home to steadily achieve those goals. I learned how to manage my finances, and discovered what credit was and how to maintain good credit. I learned to write checks for the first time in my life and balance my checkbook.

The concept of credit was new to me and not a thing I grew up with in Somali culture. (We'll cover credit in depth in a later chapter.) Using credit wisely (the process of acquiring something you need or want right now and paying for it in small increments over time) is a significant part of succeeding in the U.S. I learned that I can use the credit element of American culture to help me have a better life–I also learned how credit can harm us when we don't use it well or we trust people we shouldn't with our credit. I learned about collection agencies and how to negotiate with them.

I learned how to save money and the importance of saving money. Lutheran Social Services through Thrivent Bank had a 4-to-1 savings match program. If you save a dollar, they give you four dollars. If you save a hundred dollars, they give you four hundred dollars. Within the two-year program, if you're consistent, every month that you save fifty dollars, they match two hundred dollars. So it motivates you to reach the financial goals you set for yourself.

Then my family caseworker encouraged me to go back to school and get the education I needed to get a better job. And have a better income for my family. I started going to school at Minneapolis College. It took me a while, but I was able to register and get my associate degree in business management, which is a two-year degree.

Goals require help.

It is critical for anyone who has goals and dreams to have someone to help them. It can be an organization, a coach, or a mentor.

Once you set goals for yourself, it's crucial to get the right help in achieving them. Imagining where you want to go in your life is one thing, but it's hard to stay inspired if you can't see how your dreams can become real. Or what steps you must take each day to make them happen. Achieving my goals has been a slow process of hundreds of tiny steps—small changes I've made to my life each day, week, month, and year to get where I want to go. I needed guidance and suggestions to know which tiny step to take next.

If someone had told me when I first arrived in Minnesota that I needed or even *could* go to college, I would never have believed it! How ridiculous! It was only after learning a new language, getting on my feet financially, and feeling a growing sense of safety and stability that I could realistically consider higher education.

Without the help of Community Action in Minnesota (https://caphennepin.org/), I would not have been able to accomplish the things that I accomplished. Through Community Action, I met my mentor and friend Mickey

Mikeworth, who has been in my life ever since, who has helped me so much and inspired me to become a better person.

Goals require time.

Mickey is the one who taught me to look at time management from the perspective of one hour or one half-hour at a time. Here's how it works: Everyone has twenty-four hours. One thing that we all have equal amounts of is time. No matter who we are, we all have twenty-four hours.

It's how we use those twenty-four hours. Mickey told me to break my day into thirty-minute increments. Everything I need to do, I do in thirty-minute increments.

This is my calendar:

From 5:00am to 5:30, I wake up, pray and meditate.

From 5:30 to 6:00 a.m. each day, I cuddle with my two youngest children. I wake up, we cuddle for thirty minutes, then I get them ready for school for thirty minutes.

After that, I walk, then I read, and then I write, taking thirty minutes for each task. Then I get ready for work at 8:00 a.m.

My workday is also divided into thirty-minute increments, working, taking breaks, and having meetings. And in this way, my calendar is nearly full and with no wasted time. I also have reserved time for myself and for personal growth. I'm continually setting new goals because I've created space in my busy life to manifest my dreams—one half-hour at a time.

Notice how everything I've achieved happened slowly. You have to be aware that change is not easy. Sometimes when we start to change our lives, your immediate family or community may not support you. They may not understand what you are trying to accomplish.

You must find the people who will support you (like Mickey did for me.) When you have this support outside yourself, it will be so much easier to make changes inside yourself and stick to your path. Only share your vision with people who can:

- Guide you
- Coach you

- Mentor you
- Support you
- Enrich you
- Nourish you

Ultimately, share your vision only with people who want you to succeed! Coaches, mentors, motivational speakers, and other people with inspiring stories of change and growth can all help you find your strength and keep taking action on your goals.

It is an absolutely worthwhile investment of time and energy to find community or online resources to teach you essential life skills like time management and financial knowledge, and then dedicate the time required to learn the skills. Because, just like listening to your Inner Voice and your Angels, it's investing in yourself. Respecting yourself.

My mentor and friend Mickey Mikeworth has graciously agreed to share the goal setting and time management process she taught me with readers of this book. Please enjoy her wisdom and experience:

Mickey Mikeworth:

Time management means how you actually activate your life. The most important part of time management and financial management is understanding the resource "flow" and how *magnification* works. (Magnification means to intensify something or make it bigger.)

The most important principle is understanding that *time* is your most precious resource. We love to think it's money. But *time* is where you actually get to build your wealth. The reason you want to protect and manage your time is because that's how you build your fortune. *Time management is the tool.*

Once you have agency—which is the ability to actively approach a goal, the belief that you can do something, that you have the power to do something—that means that you have will, or determination and purpose.

Agency then requires action.

That's when we get into time management. Time management is the tool with which you learn the lesson of boundaries. The purpose of boundaries is actually to keep something in, not to push something away. So the first thing that we learn about time management is the purpose of a boundary.

If I wanted to demonstrate the purpose of a boundary, I would give you a cup and a pitcher of water. And I would ask you to start to fill the cup with water and say, a boundary is something that holds something. Like this cup is holding water.

When you're putting a boundary around time, you're doing so because you want something to fill that cup. You're creating space for something. Then imagine if I put some water in another cup. And tossed that cup of water at the outside of the cup that you're holding.

I would say, "This is the most *inefficient* use of a boundary, right?" Because a lot of times we think, let me put up this boundary so nothing can come in. *That's the worst boundary you could have.*

What you want to understand is that a boundary is a cup and it's a cup that you fill. The reason you're putting a boundary around time is because you want to fill that cup with actions, actions that build your wealth. Think about putting the actions *inside* your cup that build wealth.

If you want to build the wealth of your family, then you put quality time with your children, husband, or parents and siblings in your cup. If you're trying to build the wealth of your community, then put your community action and efforts in there. If you're trying to build the wealth of you as a person, then put the time that you need for yourself inside your cup.

The purpose of a boundary is the first lesson in time management. But in order to be able to create boundaries, you first have to have desire and agency. After that, you must take action. Action is about movement.

It's about making a small change. It's about a game plan. It's about mobilizing. It's about taking calculated risk. It is the ability to take agency and energy together, right? It's saying, *I have the will to change my life. And I have the ability to change my life. And then I have to give energy to it.*

Desire + energy = action.

Then we have this ability to start making dreams come true.

Because we have a list of things that we want done, accomplishments or things that we want in our life, now we can just start plugging them in. The advice I give people is this: start with 2% of your time. 2% of your time is 28 minutes each day. It's a half hour.

So you have to take 2% of your time every day to say, I'm going to put 2% of my time towards the things that are most meaningful to me. And that will magnify in the ways that I want.
To do that, you have to have a little bit of strategy. A lot of times that's just learning when things are coming up in your life.

For example, you know what bills are due and when they're due right? Part of time management is knowing when people are going to ask for your time. When people are going to ask for your resources.

Because time is just one of many resources, but it is the one that is actually the most precious to you. So on a calendar, knowing what time somebody is going to ask you for money (like your rent or your phone and utility bills), how much *time* do you have to work for that money?

You can ask, do I actually need the time exchange in money, or do I need a *resource exchange* in money? (A resource exchange is something other than money you can use to get what you need.)

This perspective helps with time management as well. Because then you can see that it may be that you need to take the time to go apply online for local daycare assistance in your region to access that resource because *daycare assistance* will now pay the bill. In that case, investing the time to secure daycare assistance is a better use of time than working the number of hours that would be required to earn the money to pay the daycare bill.

And this is where we start to break the illusion that everything requires money. It does not. *Everything requires time.*

As you become wealthier, you start to realize that you can actually *magnify your wealth by buying your time or buying another person's time.* Like, paying someone to fix your car rather than taking the time to learn how to fix your own car.

In other words, it takes less time for you to pay another person for how they've used their time. So, understand that time is the most precious resource! And the reason that you're managing it isn't because you just want to be more efficient and get more done and have a longer task list, it's so you can maximize your wealth and satisfaction.

You have to understand that time is your biggest resource because it is your most precious commodity. And then we will craft the vision and the voice and the leadership around what we are trying to build in our life.

That is what time management is. It is vision, voice, and leadership. And the faster that you can partner with those concepts, the faster you'll start building wealth and achieving your goals and dreams.

How to begin setting goals and taking action

As we build on the previous chapters and you experiment with the tips in them, you may be noticing some differences in your life, even if they are tiny. Perhaps after finding a few moments of alone time each week, you've been able to discover and listen to your Inner Voice and your Angel Guides. Here's what to try next:

- Start noticing your desires as they pop up. (These desires could be big and seemingly impossible, like owning a new house, or small and manageable like wanting to try a new restaurant for lunch.)
- Write down three desires you have this week.
- Choose one of the more immediate and manageable desires (for example, you'd like to get an afternoon of childcare for your kids, so you can go on a walk and run errands by yourself, or you've always wanted to start your own business.)
- If your goal is to start a business, think about the type of work you're passionate about—if you did that work for 24 hours straight, it would still be a deep joy to do it.
- Choose the day or approximate timeline in which you'd like this desire to become reality. (Such as, *"I want to have a babysitter for next Thursday from 1pm to 5pm."*, or *"I will launch my business by this time next year.")*
- Take the next action to make your new goal happen. (Call around to your friends to see if they are available to watch your children, or know someone trustworthy who could babysit. Or, research local agencies that can help you write a business plan and secure funding.)

Getting practice setting smaller goals and taking action on them helps you feel comfortable setting larger goals that take longer to achieve. As you practice goal-setting and action, you'll also get practice managing your time and setting the boundaries you need to ensure that your time is filled up with only the actions that get you closer to your goals.

My Dear Sister, this is how I move forward in my life continually. You don't have to do it all alone. Goal-setting is a never-ending practice that expands and enriches your life. By the way, you cannot fail at this practice. Sometimes you may not reach your goals. Think of that setback as your Angels gently letting you know that direction wasn't meant for you, and to keep setting goals that you can achieve.

Questions to help you learn to set goals to prioritize and manage your time:

- What is your life's purpose at this time in your life?

____

____

____

____

____

____

- What is the one most important thing you can do right now to create space in your life to dream, set and prioritize goals, and then make them happen?

____

____

____

____

____

____

____

____

- Do you have a one-year goal? A three-year goal? (The goal could be for your education/ career, your finances, your spiritual or family life, etc.)

- What are the first three steps you need to take to reach your goal?

~~~

My Powerful Sisters, as you are reading this chapter, I would encourage you to reevaluate your life, your goals, and your dreams. I would like you to know what is important to you in this life. My goal for you is that you really look at your life very closely and change what is necessary.
~~~

Chapter 5

Take Care of Your Emotional Health

One of the most difficult aspects of my life that I am still struggling with is my mom choosing her husband (my stepdad) over me. She abandoned me because she felt like she had no choice.

When I had just moved to America, there was a family argument about whether my husband and I could assist my stepfather with a family immigration issue. When we were unable to help, my stepfather gave my mom an ultimatum: *"Either force your daughter to help me and my other family, or I'll divorce you."*

My stepfather had abused me in so many different ways and he made her choose him over me. He used his military background to manipulate and threaten her. He said, *"I'm going to divorce you if you choose Fatoun. If you choose her over me, I will divorce you."* She felt like she had no choice, because she depended on him for her survival.

My sister called our mom last year and said, *"I just want to know why a mother would choose a man over her daughter? And why did you treat Fatoun the way you treated her?"*

My mom said that she had to choose her husband because she had younger children to take care of and couldn't survive on her own. She was an immigrant. She didn't speak the language. She didn't know how to drive. She had a family to feed.

As a stranger in her new land, she didn't know the environment, the culture, the people, or the language. She didn't know who or how to ask for help. Since she could not drive, she wouldn't be able to take the children to school, buy groceries, or do anything if her husband divorced her. She was stuck. Like she had no choice.

And her thinking was, since I was her oldest child and already married, it was easier to disconnect me from her life and choose her husband so she could take care of the younger children.

He covered up the abuse I endured at his hands. He isolated her by coming between her and her sister, and cutting her off from my life completely.

It took her over twenty years to realize that his manipulation, his deception, and his abuse were affecting everybody around her. He not only made my mom choose him over me, he made sure that none of my siblings had contact with me.

It was only when his abusive and deceptive behavior affected my mother directly that she woke up. This happened when, one day, my stepfather returned to Somalia and remarried his first wife. He hid his remarriage from my mom. My mom realized then that he was turning his back on her, and she asked him for a divorce. To hear her tell it, he made her life miserable after that, attempted to physically harm her, and sued her for money. He did grant her a divorce, but made it nearly impossible for her to leave with her good reputation and safety intact.

I coped with the emotional pain of my mom choosing her husband over me by numbing myself to it. I buried my feelings for many, many years because I didn't know how to deal with them.

There's a huge, huge cultural-emotional burden on Somali and other women and even children. You cannot disobey your family. You cannot speak back. You cannot question certain things. Your parents are your parents no matter what and you cannot disagree with them or cut off communications with them. So it was really extremely difficult for me when I was surrounded by Somali women or families and watched them having a loving relationship with their mothers and with their siblings. I felt deeply depressed and isolated because of that.

I felt very lonely. I had no relationships. I was alone in this world. I grew up without a father. I never saw my father. I craved the love, affection, and protection of him every day. There was a deep empty hole in my heart that was longing for a caring, responsible man who nurtured my soul.

My mom, who traveled extensively when I was small for the family import/export business, came back into my life after she married her second husband when I was seven years old.

When I started living with my mom, my only memories are of her beating me up, yelling at me, pulling my hair, ordering me to do stuff. She does not want to talk about the past, she does not want to apologize for what she did, she does not want to admit what happened was wrong, and she does not want to heal and build a better future. She wants to pretend nothing happened and just act normal. It is very hard for me to act normal when I don't even know what normal is.

She wasn't a nurturing mom. She wasn't a loving mom. She never hugged me, held me, or told me that she loved or cared for me. I never felt wanted by my mother, I always felt invisible around her.

And then civil war broke out in Somalia. We had to move to a refugee camp, and we stayed there for many years—over a decade. In the refugee camp, life was not easy.

But then my mom sent me away to the refugee camp to live with strangers that I didn't know anything about.

I had always felt deeply unwanted. I felt like I was an outsider, like I didn't belong to my family. I didn't get the emotional nourishment that I needed as a child. There was always a void in my heart–an empty spot–where I longed for family, a nurturing family, a loving family, a loving mother. She wasn't there. Nobody ever was.

My mom and I were able to reunite in my early 20s. I felt like, *"Oh, now I have my mom in my life!"* That's when my stepdad made sure that I had no relationship with her, so that he could cover up the abuse I survived.

This was a devastating low point for me. And then I felt like, *"Why am I even here? What is family about?"*

And at forty-eight years old, I *still* feel lonely, alone, not loved by my family. I have to live with that. I have to learn how to cope with it by reading a lot of information and believing that I'm here for a purpose.

I am here because I have four beautiful children. I can give them things that I didn't have with my mother, with my siblings. I show my kids love, kindness. I give them conversation, affirmations, cuddling, hugs, and emotional support. I teach them right from wrong, tell them stories, I'm present with them. Because of me, they have structure in life, faith, and education. Everything I never had as a child, I make sure they have with me.

Finally, when my mom found out what kind of person my stepdad was, she came back into my life. Today, I believe that my mom was afraid of him. In my heart, I believe that my mom was a victim as well. But she pretends like the abuse didn't happen and she doesn't want to talk about it.

I still can't make sense of her reluctance to share in this truth with me. Our talks are brief and they stay on the surface. Our conversations sound like *"How are you, how's life, how's your health?"* Until she's ready to talk about what happened to me, I cannot have a healthy relationship with her. I hope one day we can heal this deep wound between us.

Healing the feelings

For the first ten years I was in Minneapolis, I would cry and sob. All of the loss of family and everything I survived to get to Minnesota on my own was all just too painful to hold in.

I was deeply, deeply wounded from my neglectful childhood, from an abusive marriage, from moving across the world, from living in a war-torn country, from fleeing violence all the time. I needed time, self-care, and the care of others to come out of that. I knew there was a higher purpose for me. I decided I needed to do something to help me start to move through my emotional pain.

So often I have seen people cope with pain or sadness or depression in self-destructive ways like using drugs, excessive partying, or looking for validation and love in the wrong ways or with the wrong people. I knew there had to be a better approach, but I needed help finding it.

I went to my doctor and told her how I was feeling. And my doctor told me that it sounded like I was depressed and lonely. She said I had two choices. One was to take medication to help me relax, ease my depression, and sleep. The other choice was to *find a therapist to talk with about my grief and find ways I could cope and get better.*

I didn't want to take medication, which a lot of people do. It's an easy way out to take medication, but I didn't want to be addicted to medication and I didn't want to be numb. I didn't want to feel like a zombie. I was a mother of two young children. I wanted to be alert and awake and be aware and help them have a better life. I wanted to work. **So I chose the therapist.**

The therapist listened to my story and she gave me tips. She said, *"You know, after listening to you talk about your childhood and what you went through, there's a five-year-old girl inside of you that is crying out for validation, for love, for a mother figure, for a nurturing mother."*

She said, *"You can nurture that child within you, nurture that child within you through your children."* That was powerful for me. I gave all my children all the hugs, the love, the affection, the cuddling that I needed from my mother. Basically I was getting what I needed through my children. My therapist suggested other things that would also help me: walking, eating better, getting plenty of sleep, exercising. These practices all helped me feel stronger and healthier.

My advice to mothers is, *please don't ever choose a man over your (child) children, because men come and go. You can always find a man, you will never forgive yourself for disowning your children for a man, and you could lose your child forever.*

How to Get and Stay Emotionally Healthy

The journey to emotional health is also a practice. Changes happen gradually, and help from others you trust is crucial to feeling better. Try these tips as a starting point:

- If you're numb, deeply sad, rageful, or feeling so low you can't seem to pull yourself up, tell yourself the truth. You are not okay right now, but you can be with help.
- Visit your doctor and ask for a referral for a therapist.
- Medication can be helpful at first or it might not be for you–talk to your doctor about your options and to help you make a decision that is right for you.
- Get over the cultural stigma of seeking help. You are valuable. Your feelings count. Your healing is important. You are not weak.
- Remember that even though your emotions can seem overwhelming and scary sometimes, they are temporary and you will survive. *The only way to heal is to feel.* Having mental health support is crucial.
- You CAN feel better, find joy, and look forward to better times.

Questions to help you learn to take care of your emotional health:

- Do you often feel empty inside? And drained emotionally? Do you run out of energy most days?

  ____

  ____

  ____

  ____

- Are there simple practices you can make part of each day, like walking, eating better, getting plenty of sleep, exercising, that will help build a foundation of healthy living and increased energy?

- Are you willing to talk to your doctor about your emotional health and try therapy if recommended? Or try journaling, affirmations, and other simple but powerful positive steps that you can take?

~~~

My Resilient Sisters, as I write this message to you, I am feeling so many emotions and I am praying to Allah to ease any pain you are struggling
~~~

with. Sometimes, it feels dark and lonely out there, but I promise that things will get better. You are strong. You are amazing. You are powerful. You can successfully navigate tough times and arrive at a place of peace and healing.

Chapter 6

Take Care of Your Mental Health

In order for me to do the work I do, I have to live in the present moment, not the past. I had an identity crisis for so long because of my mother's rejection and my father's absence and all the hardships I went through.

I didn't receive love or compassion from my family until I had my children to love and care for. I was not educated in my Islamic religion, not educated in any academic tradition, not an American, and discriminated against in my own Somali community because of my minority tribe heritage. I felt unwanted and unloved on all sides for many years.

I've often thought, "*Who am I and why am I here? Where do I belong?*"

I can't live in the past because if I dwell on what happened to me and the difficulties and losses in my life, I wouldn't do the work I'm doing. I can't focus on the things I *don't* have in my life. Instead, I'm focusing on what I *do have.* I'm focusing on healing. I am focusing on the people I love, the people that love me and show me love, and the people that accepted me and nurtured me.

Fifteen years ago, when I was seeing a therapist, that was something that people in my community didn't do. Too often, they still don't. People say, *"If you're seeing a therapist, you must not be okay. You must be losing your mind. You must be unwell. And worse than that, you must have a weak faith. You're not close to Allah (God). So shame on you for feeling the way you're feeling. You're just ungrateful!"*

But feeling sad and depressed has *nothing* to do with faith!

I was going to my therapists and counselors all the time for despair and depression. And therapy was really beneficial as a starting point in healing; first steps. Then I found something else that really helped me, deeply, truly helped me. I came up with it on my own: self-talk.

I started to journal to my soul. My dear, loving soul. Journaling helped me heal.

I talked to my soul like it was a friend. I started a journal where I asked myself questions like: *How can I help you, my dear soul?* Journaling was really helpful to me, talking to my own soul as a person. Asking my soul how the day went, what's making me upset, how I can help, and getting advice from my soul. And telling my soul that I was powerful and everything was going to be okay.

I wrote to my soul, "This is what I want today, and I will make a promise: we're going to do this together."

I treated my soul like talking to a friend. *"Okay, let's do this. Let's get a spa day. Let's go for a walk."* In my journal, it was okay to say, *"I wish I had a mom in my life, but I don't have one."*

When I was feeling sad about being abandoned by both my mom and my dad and being here in this world alone, I could also tell myself that there are other people who have it worse. I have my health, I'm in a safe country, I can work, I'm getting an education, and I can think outside the box. I can give myself affirmations and reminders of the wonderful things that I have in my life: beautiful children (even though it's not easy to be a single parent.) I have resources. Imagine those women back at home in Somalia that don't have any resources!

Feeling sad and then talking to my soul and journaling about my conversation was a way of coping, of soothing and encouraging myself, reminding myself that I have opportunities, and I can change my life. Not only my life, but also other people's lives!

This practice of journaling (along with my therapist) got me going in another direction besides depression and sadness.

I also heard Dr. Verna Price speak at a seminar offered by St. Catherine University in Saint Paul, Minnesota. (Dr. Price is the author of four books, including *The Power of People: Four Kinds of People Who Can Change Your Life*. The affirmations are from the *Girls Taking Action* curriculum book.)

A friend of mine had invited me to go with her to the seminar. As Dr. Price was speaking, her power and energy and her message resonated so completely with my mind and my soul that I thought, I've got to meet this woman.

I bought her book, but my gut instinct was telling me I needed to meet her in person. I found her email address and tried to email her a few times. But I kept deleting the emails because I was scared and nervous and didn't feel comfortable sending her an email. I was afraid that this powerful woman wouldn't have time or energy for me.

Then I decided to call her, hoping that she wouldn't answer the phone, but she did. And I was nervous and scared but I told her that I would like to meet her for tea and get to know her and see how she could help me.

She said, *"Sure, let's make an appointment."* So we had tea and she's been in my life ever since then, which was around 2011! I was so glad I took the risk to reach out.

Since then Dr. Price has been my mentor, my coach, my support, and a friend to my family. Through the nonprofit organization I founded, SomFam (short for Somali Youth and Family Development Center), I have become one of the women who mentors girls in her organization Girls Taking Action, the East African Chapter. I have invited Dr. Price to speak at book clubs and events because I believe her message is so important for women to hear.

When I read Dr. Price's affirmations each day, in the beginning, I couldn't believe the kind words I said to myself. My mind didn't want to believe that I was lovable, that I was important, that I was valuable, that I was extremely powerful.

It was hard for me to believe that I was beautiful. It was hard for me to believe that I was valuable. It was hard for me to believe that I was lovable. Any kind of healthy affirmation was hard for me to believe and to receive. I never grew up hearing kind words about myself. I didn't even know they existed because of the critical and often negative language of my upbringing and culture.

My family and some of my community have a harsh, harsh way of parenting. The only affirmation my people have is to compare you to someone who is better than you—and say, "*Why can't you be more like them*?" (Thinking that the question will motivate someone to become a better person.)

I read Dr. Verna Price's book and I practiced the affirmations until they stopped sounding awkward and untrue. The affirmations are really powerful. They have changed me. Now I wholeheartedly believe them. I read them to my girls. I read them to myself.

Here is the affirmation that was most transformative for me (which Dr. Price gave permission to include here):

WHEN I WAS BORN

When I Was Born, I Was Born Valuable!
When I Was Born, I Was Born Important!
When I Was Born, I Was Born Lovable!
When I Was Born, I Was Born Powerful!
And No Matter What ANYONE Has Said About Me,
No Matter What ANYONE Has Done To Me,
No Matter What I Have Said About Myself,
No Matter What I Have Done To Myself,
I AM Still Valuable! I AM Still Important!
I AM Still Lovable! I AM Still EXTREMELY Powerful!
© Dr. Verna Cornelia Price

Now I believe the affirmations, but it took me so, so long to feel comfortable even saying them out loud. Affirmations helped me learn how to disassociate from everything that was negative, whether it was family, friends, neighbors, what I listened to, what I read.

I want to tell you it's a learned technique. Once you learn how to do it, if you feel a negative thought coming, you can stop it immediately and turn it into a positive thought right away. One of the things that I'm really good at is being positive with my friends. They call me and say *How are you, Fatoun*?

I say, "*Oh, I'm doing great!*", and I mean it. Those words automatically come out now.

"How's your day?"

"Wonderful, amazing."

My friends say, "*Oh, tell me what's amazing?*"

Responding this way is a habit of creating something positive to say when somebody greets you. I love it. I remember walking into Galleria Mall one day and I saw an old friend who was dragging and slacking. He was with a white woman who was working for him.

I was so happy. I greeted him and he said, *"How are you doing?"*

I said, *"I'm doing great; excellent."*

And the woman with him said, *"I want to be on whatever she's on."*

He said, *"Well, you seem so happy and excited. What's going on?"*

I said," *Nothing! I'm just happy. Life is full of possibilities and I'm high on life and the beautiful, amazing breath that we're taking. It's fresh, we're breathing, and that is something that we take for granted. We're healthy and we're walking and we take that for granted."*

His companion said, *"Wow, I didn't see that."*

Within my own community, people don't know what I went through. So they always see me happy, excited, and carrying myself well. They always wonder why I'm the way I am. They don't know that I made a decision to create a better way of living for myself.

Because therapy was so important in my healing, I recommend it as a starting point for anyone struggling with depression or despair. If you don't resonate with the first therapist you try, then find another. You may connect with some therapists and not with others. Don't give up!

You may prefer to seek out a therapist, for example, who's older and has a lot of life experience. You can also base your choice of therapist on the kinds of issues you're going through. Is it postpartum depression? Marriage or family counseling? Work issues? You can do research online and see what areas each therapist specializes in.

I've seen a lot of therapists and what I have learned is that therapists are human beings. For example, a brand new therapist just out of university or a young White therapist would never understand my story and my life.

They would try to guide me based on what they know, but their life experiences would have been so different from mine that I gain much more from therapy with someone with whom I share some common experiences. Once you find a therapist that you feel comfortable with, they'll truly listen to you and give you valuable resources and support and guidance.

Hodan Farah on Mental Health and Childhood Trauma

Hodan Farah is a social worker in Ottawa, Canada. She works extensively with immigrants and specializes in healing childhood trauma. Enjoy her wise words about seeking mental health:

Childhood trauma often refers to traumatic experiences that occurred during one's early years. Many women living in Western countries have experienced war or various forms of violence at a young age, and they still bear the scars of this war. Black immigrant women, whether directly or indirectly, have often experienced some form of trauma. As far back as I can remember from my own childhood, Black women have endured significant violence (sexual or physical, psychological neglect).

During her youth, a woman's position in the family is often lower than that of her brothers. Yet, this same woman or girl is expected to take care of everything—cleaning, cooking, looking after younger siblings. Her opinion does not matter; she gets beaten by her brothers, cousins, or uncles for daring to say no or for expressing her opinion. She wasn't allowed to go out without permission. Some girls are forcibly married at a very young age, experiencing difficult childbirths for which their bodies were not prepared, which results in trauma.

Recognizing the signs of childhood trauma is challenging because the person who has experienced it often does not realize they have trauma, and they unknowingly pass it on. Childhood trauma shapes the lives in a way of seen and unseen. It becomes a deep wound in the psyche. It affects the thought, the behavior and the relationships(with yourself or with others). Addressing this wound is significantly important for healing, as unresolved trauma can manifest in many ways (anxiety, fear, distress, mental health is a taboo subject in our cultural communities, trauma is a part of mental health.)

In cultural communities, the weight of cultural and spiritual belief systems influences the reluctance to seek out Western healthcare systems. In some cultures, mental illness is seen as a mystical issue (fatalism, witchcraft, spirits) or tied to perceptions of misfortune (guilt, sin, fate).

First, it is important to note the cultural differences in the perception of mental illness. Research shows that these cultural differences limit people from seeking the formal support they need. In Western countries, the perception of mental health has significantly evolved over time. People with mental disorders are no longer locked away in psychiatric asylums or considered "crazy." Today, these individuals receive a diagnosis (depressive, bipolar, schizophrenic).

The history of mental illness in racialized immigrant communities is characterized by invisibility, labeling, and marginalization. In terms of invisibility, the history of illness is a coded history, filled with silence, unspoken truths, and traces that always need to be deciphered and interpreted with knowledge. Labeling also occurs as society imposes a label on the individual. The person loses their identity and assumes an identity imposed by society (labeling).

Faced with prejudice and the resulting consequences (rejection, social isolation, humiliation, etc.), people or their relatives often try to control information about their mental health or that of their loved ones for fear of being judged, stigmatized, or rejected by others. They must hide their psychological distress to appear normal in front of others, leading to stigmatization, discrimination, and a lack of adequate vocabulary to express what they feel. Their integrity and personhood are violated by giving them nicknames (buufis or waswas in Somali language).

The Importance for Women to Take Care of Their Mental Health

Women are the pillars of the household; when a woman falls ill, it is often noticed within her home. It is crucial for women to take care of themselves first.

To do this, women must seek the necessary help. It is important to turn to people with whom they share a cultural affinity or a relationship of trust, such as professionals or ethnic and cultural communities. In Western countries, women can have the opportunity to find therapies that can help them feel better, but for them to seek out this therapy, they must first recognize the need for mental health care, just as one would for physical health. Specifically, recognizing and accepting that mental health needs to be prioritized. Women need to support each other in seeking mental health help. Often, women turn to their friends to discuss their distress, which is not a bad thing, but they also need to turn to a mental health expert to receive the necessary help.

Recommendations

- *It is important to serve people in their native language, as this facilitates clear communication for establishing an accurate diagnosis and implementing an appropriate treatment plan, especially in mental health care. Furthermore, the literature supports that intervention should take place in the patient's native language to allow them to express their emotional pain in their own language.*

- *Consult a health expert who speaks their language or has a healthcare translator available.*
- *Understanding the impact of the trauma involves recognizing its presence and how it influences the daily interactions and choices. Therapy can be a transformative tool to unpack the past under the guidance of expertise.*
- *Healing trauma doesn't mean erasing your past, but changing your relationship with your memories. It means learning a way to cope with it, building resilience, and often reconstructing our self , our identity. The journey requires patience, courage, and support from loved ones and professionals.*
- *Celebrating small victories. Healing is not quick, but each step forward is a step reclaiming your life. Allow yourself grace on the tough moments and recognize that each moment of therapy or self-care is a brick in the foundation of a healing journey.*
- *Asking for help can provide valuable information, ease your burden, give you support, and help you find a path to feeling better.*
- *Listen to your body's signs (lack of sleep, intense fatigue, anxiety) and prioritize self-care.*
- *Speak positively about yourself because our brain often records and internalizes negative information.*
- *Build a healthy relationship with yourself and others.*
- *Encourage a community of understanding of mental health, by sharing your journey of healing. It's not comfortable to talk about your mental health, but you can be the one who breaks the taboo. You can inspire, enlighten, and offer hope to other women who might feel isolated in the struggle, but want to heal, grow and transform their pain into strength.*

How to ease your mental burden this week:

As with every other topic we've covered, improving your mental health is a practice–a journey. Here are several actions you can do this week to start feeling lighter, more empowered, and joyful in your mind and body.

- Go for a walk. Even a short walk in nature can help you feel calm and centered. When we move our bodies, we produce "happy" hormones called endorphins. These brain chemicals can lift our mood and help us find a taste of happiness. Plus, moving your body in any way is free and simple.
- Begin looking for a therapist. You can search online for mental health professionals, counselors, and therapists in your area. You can ask your friends, colleagues, or coworkers for recommendations.
- Start repeating one affirmation to yourself out loud this week. Choose one from the affirmation above, or create a positive statement you can tell yourself that you can come to believe, even if you don't believe it today.

Questions to help you learn how to take care of your mental health:

- When you are alone with your thoughts, can you ask yourself questions? Do you have the courage to be honest with yourself?

____

____

____

____

____

____

____

- Do you feel safe enough at home to write to your soul and have conversations with yourself? To set goals, based on what you discover or learn?

- Can you learn to love, respect, and value yourself and appreciate the unique lovable person you are? Are you brave enough to take baby steps?

~

My Beautiful, Valuable, Loving Sisters, I want you to know that you are powerful beyond whatever you went through or whatever you are going through at this moment. Know that your past does *not* define who you are and it does *not* limit your potential of who you can become. Life is all about growth and learning.

Chapter 7
Take Care of Your Physical Health

As long as I can remember, there were certain foods that I didn't like to eat. Every time I tried to eat them, my body didn't like it. For example, butter. And goat ghee. (Any animal fat, really.) Also, my body didn't like sweets.

In Somalia, my grandparents had an orchard. We ate a lot of cabbage, potatoes, carrots, soups, and lean meat in those soups. As soon as I started walking, I would go into the orchard and I would eat fruits. I ate all day! I ate fruits and vegetables, carrots, grapes, oranges, apples…So I grew up eating healthy as a child.

When we ate our injera bread in the morning, people used to have it with eggs. But I hated the taste of eggs and the smell of eggs. I didn't like any dairy products whatsoever. I couldn't eat and drink milk.

When I was around four to six years old, my mom hired a lady who milked goats to make sure I had plenty of milk because I was so skinny. (My mom traveled for the work she did for my grandparents' import/export business so she wasn't around me; she wasn't living with us.) The woman would call me, take me under a tree, and make me drink the goat milk. She would force me to drink it. I remember throwing up. I would gag and throw up. I hated that.

Then my mom came back after she remarried. I was seven years old and she would beat me because I wouldn't eat animal fats, like butter. I was too skinny and we didn't have a lot of food. We were very poor after my mom remarried because her parents had kicked her out. They didn't approve of her marriage and made her stop working for them. My siblings and I were kicked out at that time also.

Because of my specific tastes in food, I didn't have much to eat. I was too skinny and she didn't want us to starve. So when she could get fat–animal fat–she would force me to eat it and she would beat me with wire or cords if I refused.

It was so painful! I would force myself to eat. I hated the smell and the taste. What came of that was me throwing up all over the place. Because my body was craving fruits and vegetables; that's what made me feel good. Nourished.

So for me, healthy eating and prioritizing what felt good to eat started with those horrible early experiences. I was never one to eat fried food or animal fat or dairy products until I got pregnant.

In America when I was pregnant, the doctors told me, "You have to have milk, you have to have calcium." That's how I learned that we need calcium for strong bones and to grow healthy babies. I would close my nose and swallow so I didn't smell the milk!

When I was living out in California, my children and I were able to have lots of fresh fruits and veggies because I was a single mother. I was married, but my husband didn't provide for us. So I worked at my job and the county also helped us. I bought fruits and vegetables with food stamps. We ate well because of my background in healthy eating and the willingness to get help affording those same foods. I believe you are what you eat.

In the Somali community, we eat a lot of bread, rice, pasta, sugar in everything, sugary drinks, sodas, oil, and meat. There are not a lot of fruits and vegetables in our daily meals. But what I learned is because of the lifestyle of my people, we have young people in their 40s, 50s, and older with diabetes, high cholesterol, high blood pressure, and insomnia.

Diabetes and other conditions mean that as a culture, we can't sleep well. We're constipated. We can't walk or exercise easily. I saw my mom suffering with diabetes, high cholesterol, obesity, and joint problems. I thought, *"You know what? I don't want to be miserable and in pain and have so many medical issues."*

Our bodies need movement, physical movement. We can start by walking. Making time for a daily walk was an intentional decision I made. Before I started doing so, I was going to my therapists and counselors all the time for despair and depression.

Even though I don't eat a lot of junk food (because I'm not a junk food eater), I ate rice and I ate bread and I drank a lot of coffee with milk. I gained weight and was not comfortable with my body. That's when the doctors told me to walk, just walk—twenty minutes walking, thirty minutes walking, whatever I could do.

I fell in love with walking because it was simple and I enjoyed it. Getting out in my neighborhood or nature helped me feel happy, just like in the tips from the last chapter! My body began changing and getting stronger. I had more energy and excitement for living. I could show up as a good parent and generous community member more often.

Then, I started dancing–like dancing in my room. I still put on my favorite music for twenty or thirty minutes and I sweat and I dance and I move! I drink plenty of water, and I learned to replace what I'm missing from food (like calcium and other nutrients) with vitamins. Many of my people–East African people–don't believe in supplementing their food diets because they think vitamins are medicine and they don't want to take pills.

Here is where I think my profound sense of isolation and loneliness has helped me live a healthier life than many of my people. Being isolated meant that I never learned the cultural messages and traditions that keep so many of us stuck. I was able to let in different knowledge that led me to a healthy body and mind, because I never learned the "old" ways of my culture. Not knowing anything in Somalia helped me make a better life in America.

The Quran: A surprising health resource

There's so much good information in the Quran. It's a beautiful, amazing guide for life. The Quran offers guidance on eating and drinking in a way that is healthy and displays respect and appreciation for our body and mind that God gave to us.

Prophet Muhammad (peace be on him) tells us that mindless eating is dangerous to our health. He instructs us to imagine our stomach with three sections: one for food, the second for water, and the third for air. If you fill your entire stomach with food, you won't have enough water to digest the food and you won't have enough space to breathe. That's why when we overeat, we feel tired. We can't breathe.

The Quran even requires Ramadan, a month-long period of cleansing through fasting and other practices. It is a time when we experience hunger and feel empathy. We help others. Ramadan is a time to restart your relationship with God.

By studying the Quran and reading articles from Islamic scholars, I have learned a lot about the physical and spiritual benefits of eating healthy foods and the importance of eating the right foods to nurture our body.

Notes on nutrition from an acupuncturist

Jesse Peterson is a licensed acupuncturist. In this traditional healing method, practitioners like Jesse look at the whole person when diagnosing and treating illness, injuries, or conditions. Here's his wisdom on nutrition:

Likewise, we have a similar problem with diet, where we've also lost touch with our traditional wisdom.

While we saw a precipitous drop in infectious disease throughout the 20th century, we saw an opposite rise in diseases of inflammation including diabetes, heart disease, asthma and allergies, and autoimmune disorders. This coincided with modern, processed foods replacing our traditional foods.

I have learned that trying to use acupuncture to heal from an injury or chronic health issue, without giving the body the nutrition that it needs is like trying to exercise with cardio and weight lifting while eating junk food. Stressing your body with exercise will require adequate sleep and better nutrition than if you're sitting around. Acupuncture also works by stressing the body, but by simulating tiny injuries to provoke a healing response.

What makes this work is the traditional practices common all over the world. Such as eating mostly warm cooked food, that is mostly meat and vegetables, limiting sugar including fruit (which was traditionally a seasonal food), detoxifying grains and beans through the traditional methods of soaking, sprouting, and fermenting (or eating root vegetables instead).

And eating liver at least once per week, which we have forgotten is the most nutrient dense food, and tried to replace it with refined and synthetic multivitamins and protein powders that don't work and cause gut problems.

Tips for eating healthier with ease

Any change takes time, as I've mentioned in all the previous chapters. Taking care of your body is no different. Try a few small changes this week and see how they feel. Sometimes you have to give a new habit a chance for 30 days or longer before it will "stick" with you.

- Go for a walk. (Yes, this was the first tip in the last chapter for mental health) Walking is a simple way to add movement to your day. Even 20 minutes will strengthen your heart and lungs and lift your mood!
- Add, don't subtract food from your diet. Instead of feeling deprived because you "can't" have rice or bread, try simply adding a fruit or vegetable to your next meal. Notice if you have less room in your stomach for the foods you want to release. Increase nutritious, high-fiber and high-protein foods over time as you develop a taste for them.

- Experiment with herbs and flavors in your cooking—make your dietary changes interesting and experimental. See which flavors you enjoy the most and make them a regular part of your weekly meals.

Questions to help you learn to take care of your physical health:

- What is your relationship to your diet and your health? Do you have any health concerns?

____

____

____

____

____

____

____

- In addition to the obvious health benefits (feeling stronger and happier, having more energy, etc.) can you view taking care of your body and mind as a way of showing appreciation for God's gift of your life? Why or why not?

____

____

____

____

____

____

____

____

____

____

- Name three ways in which your life would be different if you believed that taking care of your body and mind (through a healthy diet and exercise, taking time for yourself to rest, reflect and dream) was also a way to honor God and set a good example for your children and family.

~~~

My Dear Queens, I know that we have been struggling with eating healthy and learning a new diet plan in the U. S. One thing I have learned is you are what you eat. I know firsthand that it is not easy to change eating habits, but I also know that our bodies are our temples. The best thing we can do for our physical well being is to learn to eat healthy, exercise, and nourish our body with the right foods.
~~~

Chapter 8
Take Care of Your Spiritual Life

I fell in love with Islam when I was in college. As I mentioned in the previous chapter, the Quran is a beautiful, amazing guide for life— for praying, worshiping, family life, personal life, work life, community, and treating people with respect and dignity.

It talks about so many different expressions of respect, like respecting your partner, having respectful communication, using kind words, not harsh words. The Quran asks you to think about your words.

Other expressions of respect the Quran details are: teaching your kids good manners, respecting elderly people, being soft-spoken, and being responsible for the children that you brought to this world.

The Quran even talks about day and night. Night is for sleep, for your mind to rest, and daytime is to work and provide for your family. It tells us to live in this world like we're going to live forever but worship like it's your last day.

I fell in love with the Quran in college because I had finally had a way to read and study it. I had learned English and found a version of the Quran that was in English. I also took a class in college on the history of different world religions that opened my eyes because prophet Muhammad recognized women's rights before Western religions did. *Islam was the first major religion that affirmed the rights of women.*

According to the teachings of the Quran, women have the right to be educated. They have the right to start businesses, work, and earn their own money. They don't have to contribute to household expenses. A man asking for a woman's hand in marriage must pay a dowry to her family and then provide for their household. If she is wealthier than he is, she may choose to contribute to the household income but it's not required of her. If she gives birth to their child, she can ask her husband to pay her to breastfeed the baby because her body is producing the milk.

The prophet Muhammed (peace be upon him) was an advocate for treating women with respect in many important ways. His teachings and the way he interacted with his own wives demonstrated this belief. He was one of the first religious leaders to state that women should not be segregated during menstruation.

Mohammed (peace be upon him) also encouraged husbands to spend time with their wives, to help their wives with household work, to help and spend time with the kids, and if he could afford it, provide a housekeeper for the household.

In some cultures, the Quran is used to justify polygamy, a man having multiple wives. The Quran actually allows for multiple wives *only if the husband can treat them equally, provide for them equally, take care of them equally. He also has to have his wife's consent to marry other wives and she has to be okay with it.* Then and only then can he marry more than one woman. But if a man cannot meet these standards, having more than one wife is against the religion, it's against the Quran, because the man is incapable of providing for them.

Muslim women (Somali women) have been at a disadvantage because they were not attending their own weddings. Traditionally, the woman's husband and father are present at the wedding—women don't know what rights they have been granted in the ceremony. That is one of the ways that the tenets of Islam have been misrepresented—because women don't have access to the information of their rights under the religious laws.

Before I had access to the true teachings of the Quran (because I didn't have an education in Islam or academics,) I knew a lot of men who claimed to be imams or sheikhs or educated in Islam that made the religion seem really harsh and difficult for people. Like so many religious leaders who wanted to create and maintain power, they proclaimed, *"If you do this you're going to hell, if you do that you're going to hell, God's going to banish you..."*

It was just terrifying for me! When I was a young child, I remember being terrified of burning in hell. Because the Quran is written in Arabic, you have to speak the language in order to read it and write it and understand it. That made it easy for some to manipulate Islam and use it to control people, *especially women,* instead of educating people about the religion. Many students don't understand the meaning of the Quran, and their teachers only ask students to study, memorize, and read the Quran without teaching them the actual *meaning* of the Quran.

On top of that, in many Dugsi schools, the instructor resorts to physical violence to get children to memorize the Quran. I remember seeing children getting beaten up, with instructors even encouraging the other students to participate in the violence. It wasn't a loving environment; it wasn't even a safe environment for children to learn about Islam. Which is the exact opposite of the wisdom and gentleness contained in the Quran.

When I was a child, my mom told me that she was going to enroll me in Islamic study to learn the Quran. The school was just across the street from my house, so I had seen the sheik beat the children with a long branch, like a cane. He also beat the children with a heavy belt if they didn't recite the verses correctly.

I was so afraid! Afraid of getting beaten, pinched, mocked. Afraid because the instructor said that if you didn't follow the rules you weren't following God. And that God would banish you and you would go to hell.

I remember when my mom took me there. I was around nine years old and they gave me some words to memorize. But I couldn't memorize them because I didn't understand them. The sheik started yelling at me and I looked back at him, asking myself, "*Why is he yelling at me*?"

Instead of telling me to repeat after him or helping me understand, he yelled some more and told the other kids to beat me up. I started to run, trying to escape. I had seen what they did to other children who didn't do their homework. They tied them under the tree and pinched them. There was even a song that went with the pinching. I never went back to that Dugsi and then the civil war happened. When we got to Djibouti my mom sent me to Islamic study again. I was thirteen or fourteen years old and the teacher tried to molest me.

I never told my mom. I could not tell her. She would have beaten me up, yelled at me, forced me to go back. So I kept it quiet. My mom was working so I just stayed home and hung out with my siblings. It was only a short period of time—just a few months.

Then our situation completely changed because my stepdad came to live with us and life got really bad for us after that. The teacher that molested me didn't get in trouble because I didn't say anything. I knew my mother wouldn't believe me.

Children don't talk about the abuse because the teacher is like the second parent. So parents don't step up and advocate for their child. Bad teachers don't get in trouble. That's the thing. We only find out about teachers abusing children when something tragic happens, like when a child is severely beaten up or is molested and gets really hurt or injured. The only time parents or other adults step in is when things turn out badly.

This widespread abuse is not happening only in Somalia. Even here in Minneapolis, the teachers were following this tradition of punishing children who are struggling with the lessons! My son and daughter both told me about it. The instructor put a pen or a pencil between students' fingers and twisted it hard. Imagine punishing kids who are trying so hard to learn the Quran! As parents, we have to make sure we pay attention to our children, even when we're busy, even when we're tired. Because sometimes our kids are scared.

Some parents are really harsh. They don't listen, or might even blame the child, like the child somehow caused the problem in an abusive situation. Children are being punished by both teachers and parents, adults they should be able to trust! This is not the way to teach children about a religion that teaches the importance of respect, kindness, and responsibility. The Quran should be taught with respect and kindness and compassion so that children understand the true nature and principles of Islam.

My son saw me reading the English-language version of the Quran and asked me to buy him a copy so he could understand the meaning of what they're teaching him. They're trying to teach children to learn the Quran in Arabic, a language they don't speak or read. It's not easy to learn something in a language you don't understand, especially with the harsh teaching methods. It's very difficult to learn when you're afraid. There are amazing, good teachers out there also, but you just don't know for sure who they are until you experience them first-hand. I was fearful of my children being harmed and not wanting to continue learning or completely losing interest in Islam or the Quran.

I took my kids out of the Minneapolis Dugsi and switched to online classes. I also hired a teacher who tutors my children on the Quran at my office. That way, I know the teacher is focusing on my children and I am there. And I will only hire a teacher if they agree to this rule: if my child isn't doing well, the teacher needs to communicate their concern with words. *No physical touch and absolutely no physical discipline.*

One reason that my children enjoy online learning is because when Covid happened and everything was shut down, we found that there were Quran teachers all over the world. Currently, my children have a wonderful teacher from Kenya. Prior to that, their teacher was in Pakistan. Both teachers spoke English and kept me updated on lessons via a phone app. Many of the teachers in Minneapolis spoke Somali. And were teaching the Arabic version of the

Quran. Which made the Quran's beautiful lessons very difficult for English speaking children to learn!)

I know a lot of women who are single parents cannot afford to hire a private teacher for their children. But there are resources! There are online Islamic studies and Islamic classes. And YouTube offers a lot of educational videos on the Quran. You'll want to reach out within your community to get word-of-mouth recommendations on the best teachers and classes before getting your children started. Because the teachings of the Quran are such an important part of our children's lives, it's well worth our time and effort to find the best teachers and classes for our children.

Respecting your body and mind and soul is a way to nurture your spirituality because they are all gifts from God and you honor God when you take care of yourself. Even in a very busy life, you can create some time for yourself that nurtures your soul. Bedtime and early morning work best for me.

One thing I do is to stop eating in the evening. It keeps me awake and I toss and turn. Instead, I use this peaceful time after the children are in bed and the house is quiet to do things that nourish my spirit.

I have a kitab in English and hadiths on my bedside. So at night when I go to bed, I read the hadiths, I read the Quran, I read books that talk about Islam. I try to be in bed by nine o'clock and fall asleep by nine-thirty. So I have thirty minutes. I have the Quran and my journal next to me in bed. I read a little bit of the Quran. I journal a little bit. That's the last thing I do at night, and the first thing in the morning. I wake up at five o'clock for prayers.

While the kids are still sleeping and after morning prayers (around five o'clock, depending on when the sun rises), is a great time for me to meditate, read, relax, and do self-care. Even if you can't do it every day, making time to do so on a regular basis will create a habit of nurturing yourself and your spirit, establishing an ongoing connection to God that brings peace and inner strength to your life.

How to nourish your spirit

We've spoken so far of many simple ways to begin adding value to yourself and your life. Spirituality is another piece of becoming a whole, healthy Sister who lives a life she loves. These tips are similar to the previous chapters —repetition is the key to sustaining new habits! Practice makes progress, one day at a time.

- Choose one more block of at least 5 or 10 minutes in your day for spiritual focus.
- Read some type of spiritual literature that speaks to you, like the Quran or another soulful and thought-provoking text you're curious about.
- After reading a short segment of the book you chose, write down some of your thoughts and reflections about the passage you read. What do the words make you think or feel? Do you agree with what is said? How could you incorporate the teaching for that day into your life?

Questions to help you learn how to take care of your spiritual life:

- How do you define spirituality? What are three ways in which your spirituality impacts your everyday life?

___

___

___

___

___

___

___

___

___

___

___

- Can you envision three to five ways in which nurturing your spirituality would change your life for the better?

___

___

___

___

- What three things you can do right now to make space for and nurture your spiritual life?

~~~

My Devoted Sisters, nurturing our spirituality is not easy, but it can be done and it is a beautiful, calming feeling that our soul needs. I want you to take baby steps and connect with our creator by listening to the Quran, and reading
~~~

the Quran and the Hadiths. You will fall in love with our creator and you will become complete and content with yourself.

Chapter 9

Take Care of Your Finances

It's vitally important to understand how personal finances work in the United States, especially if you're new to the country and the U.S. financial system.

In this chapter, I will talk about what credit is and why it's important to have a high credit score, how to build credit, and how to raise a low credit score. I will also talk about how to save money, become a homeowner, and the importance of creating a will and other legal documents related to your personal finances.

How credit works

Using credit is something we're learning in the U.S., because we don't have credit back home in Somalia. Understanding credit makes living in America much easier.

Credit is leverage; the ability to get funds, buy things, or obtain services and pay for them later. If you have a credit card and pay your credit card bill in full each month, you can generally avoid paying interest, which is the (usually) high fee charged by a credit card company or financial lending institution, like a bank, to pay your bills over time. Also, most of the time, there's a high fee for credit card cash advances, so that is a credit card feature most people choose to avoid.

If you have a steady and verifiable income , you will generally qualify for a credit card and other types of loans. If you have enough money to make the payments and you have a high enough credit score, it opens up many important opportunities for you.

You can:

- buy a car.
- buy a home.
- get a loan to start a business.
- rent hotel rooms.
- rent a car.
- secure housing through rental or purchase.

It's a wake-up call for many immigrants when they try to travel, rent a hotel or a car, or rent or buy a home, to learn what a huge impact their credit score and ability to access a line of credit will have on their life. Often, this is when they first learn that they don't have a credit score.

As an immigrant new to the United States, I didn't know anything about credit until mine was messed up. A person I trusted messed it up. He was my husband at the time. He *did* know about credit and used my name and my information to apply for credit cards online without my knowledge or consent.

One day I discovered that I owed money—that I was liable—for purchases I don't know anything about! This news hit me hard. I felt betrayed, hurt, frustrated, and nearly hopeless. The whole experience was horrible and scary, and all because I only wanted to help a friend.

The first person who messed up my credit was one of my very close friends. She was a mother figure to me for a long time. I learned a painful but valuable lesson about trust and recognizing that sometimes you can't responsibly help someone, even if you'd like to.

My friend didn't mean to hurt me, but she did. She needed to rent an apartment, but couldn't. She asked me to help her, so I applied for credit and signed the apartment lease. Then she couldn't pay the rent. The next thing I knew, the apartment complex took me to court to attempt to get the rent payments she had not made, because the apartment lease had *my* name on it, not hers.

My friend called me and told me we needed to talk. She sat down with me, told me that we had to go to court, and told me what she wanted me to say. She said she would pay the bills, but she needed me to go to court because my name was on the lease.

I didn't live in the apartment. I didn't know she wasn't paying the rent. I didn't understand how doing a favor for someone so loving, kind, and generous to me could have such a damaging impact on my life. She had no idea how this would impact me either. Because I had signed this woman's lease and then she couldn't pay her rent, my credit got damaged so much that *I had trouble renting a home for myself and my family!*

These people close to you that you trust—your husband, a friend, a family member, or mentor—can make a mess of your finances without intending to. It's an easy trap to fall into because you think you're helping them and their intentions are likely good.

If someone asks you to co-sign for them on *anything*, you need to be careful because it can create expensive problems in your life, problems that can take years to recover from. I learned this the hard way.

I had the same experience with my second husband. He said, *"I'm new to the city. I don't have a job, but you have a job, and you have credit so you can buy us a car."*

"How am I going to do that?" I replied. *"I don't even have a driver's license. How am I going to pay for this?"* He told me that it would be our car and that he would make the monthly car loan payments. Since I believed we would share this car equally, I agreed to the purchase.

We went to a car dealer together. (I had never been to one before.) My husband did all the talking, and I signed up for a loan. I took out a car loan for over $30,000 in my name! I didn't fully understand the terms of the loan-like:

- how much interest I'd have to pay,
- how long I had to pay the loan back, or
- what the penalties would be if I couldn't make the loan payments.

My husband had all the power because he had a driver's license. I didn't. I didn't even know how to drive. My husband drove the car. He used the car. And he was the one who was supposed to be making the payments on the car. But he didn't.

The next thing I knew, the car was missing from the parking lot of our apartment. I thought someone had stolen it. So I called the insurance company and told them what was going on. I also called the police. That's when I found out the car had been repossessed. But I didn't know what that meant. The police officer told me that I didn't make my car payments, so the car dealer took the car back.

I was devastated. Devastated that our car was gone. Devastated that my credit score was damaged. And devastated that my husband had lied to me and betrayed my trust. I couldn't pay the money that I owed to the car dealer. My credit card score plummeted and stayed low for many, many years. It took me a long time—over a decade!— to clean up my credit and raise my score so that I could borrow money again if I needed to.

How to establish credit and keep your score high

Tip #1: Don't co-sign loans for other people, even for people you love or care about. You can simply say: *"I would like to help you, but I can't because I cannot afford to."*

The only possible exception would be loved ones for whom you are responsible
(like your children.) You might choose to cosign a loan for something that will improve their life in a meaningful and lasting way, like college or trade school. But only if you can afford to—and are willing to—*make all of the payments if you had to do so.*

Tip #2: Get a secure credit card, use less than 30% of the line of credit (money available) each month, and pay it on time.

If you're new to the country or just starting out and don't have any credit history, the first thing you can do is get a secured (pre-paid) credit card from any reputable bank using your own money. This enables you to start building a credit history with very little risk.

On your secured card, you could put as little as $200 and up to $1,000 of your own money on the card as a "line of credit." That means there is an account balance of whatever amount you put on the card. Then you use that card for purchases, pay the credit card bill on time every month, and—very important—use less than 30% of the account balance. In other words, if you have a $1,000 line of credit (because you put $1,000 of your money on the card), you'd want to use $300 or less each month.

Many people think that using the card and spending all of the money they've put on it will help their credit. It does not. It lowers the credit score if you use too much of your line of credit.

If you forget to pay your bill each month, set up auto-pay from your bank account. Connect your secured credit card to your checking account, make sure you have enough money in your checking account to pay the automatic credit card payment, and after that you can forget about it, you don't have to think about paying that bill.

Your bank teller or bank manager can assist you with setting up autopay and connecting your secured credit card to your bank account.

How to repair a low credit score

If you know your credit is messed up, whether you did it or someone else did it, the best thing you can do is get your credit report.

There's a website called www.annualcreditreport.com. Once a year, you can get a free copy (print or digital) of all the three credit reports that are issued for everyone. The three big credit reporting companies are: Equifax, Transunion, and Experian.

Once you have your credit reports, you'll still need to see your overall credit score. You'll have to pay a fee to receive your score, but you'll know what your credit score is and whether the information the credit bureaus have is accurate. Anything that you don't recognize, anything that doesn't belong to you, you can dispute.

You can write letters and dispute discrepancies. If you don't feel comfortable doing it on your own, you can go to a professional who can help you. You have to pay a fee for professional help, but having a good credit score is so important that it's worth the fee in the long run.

To dispute charges or late payments or anything that isn't accurate, you can find detailed instructions, contact information, and even template letters on this U.S. government website: www.consumerfinance.gov. Search for " How do I dispute an error on my credit report?"

You can use this URL to begin disputing any errors on your credit report: https://www.consumerfinance.gov/ask-cfpb/how-do-i-dispute-an-error-on-my-credit-report-en-314

It could take two months to resolve the dispute. It could take six months. It could take a year, depending on what issues you have. It takes time.

How to lower your interest rate and eliminate credit card interest

As you use your secured credit card and pay the monthly bill in full while making good decisions about using your credit, you can expect to raise your credit score over time. I now work in real estate and I advise anyone who wants to buy a home that they have to have good credit. A "good" credit score that qualifies you for the lowest interest rates is typically above 700. If your score is below that, it may take several months or years to raise it, depending on the cause of your low credit score.

First, you have to make sure that your secure credit card is being reported to all three credit bureaus. Then, once you have built some credit history with the bank that issued the secure credit card, you can ask the bank to convert it to a regular credit card.

The higher your credit score is, the better (lower) your interest rate is, so you're saving money in that way.

The reverse is also true: if you have a low credit score, the bank is going to charge you higher interest on your credit card because you present more of a risk. And that means you're paying more fees over time for money you borrow from the bank or finance company. So to save money, it helps in every way to have a higher credit score.

Some lenders will waive the interest fee on a credit purchase for a certain period of time if you have a high credit score **(750, or in some cases, even 700)** *and* make all your payments on time. This is usually for car loans or furniture store loans. But you have to be careful and really diligent about these offers. It's important to get all the information because often there is a high financial penalty if you are late with any payment for any reason.

These lenders often give you a "promotional" time period to pay the loan balance, and within this period, (whether it's 12, 24 or 36 months) if you make each payment on time, you won't be charged interest. In other words, you borrow money with zero fees with these offers.

Since it is a violation of Islamic religious law to pay interest, these no-interest offers can be an attractive option.

For anyone who practices Islam and lives in America, where you need to have a credit card and credit history for practically every major purchase—like a home or a car—the best thing to do is pay off your credit card's full balance each month before any interest is charged.

For example, if you charged $500 on your credit card by purchasing a new sofa, and you pay off that $500 balance before the due date (generally within 30 days), you don't pay any interest.

How to save money

Saving money is always a challenge for me since I'm a one-income household with four kids. The best way I can save money is by using a cultural tradition and service called Ayuuto. This practice of saving money is common in many countries and cultures and may be called by other names.

Ayuuto is a system of money management in which people come together in groups of (usually) ten and pool their money to create an interest-free source of money, a savings account in which each member benefits.

For example, each person contributes $2,000 each month. And each month, one member receives the entire pot of $20,000. So over the course of ten months, each of the ten group members will receive $20,000. It's a cycle.

If one person cannot afford the $2,000 monthly contribution—say they can only afford to contribute $1,000 each month—then we match them with another person with $1,000. Then when it's their turn to get the pot of $20,000, they will split it. The Ayuuto system is used in many ways, weekly, bi-weekly or monthly and it can start as little as $50, $200, $500 or more. The group has to agree on the amount and the terms.

I contribute $2,000 each month to my Ayuuto, and every ten months I will get $20,000. It works that way for each member. It's something that many Somali people (women) have done for as long as I can remember. I have been doing it for the last twenty years.

Ayuuto is a community banking system that the Somali community and some East African people use because there's no *reliable* banking system back home. People don't trust banks, but they trust community members.

The trusted community member is responsible for collecting and distributing the money plus bringing new and trustworthy people into the group. There are safeguards built into the system. If a person is new, they have to earn the trust of the other members. They'll get their money last, after all the other members have had their turn. It's a system that has worked in our culture for centuries..

Ayuuto has helped me manage my finances throughout my life. I survived by making sure I have Ayuuto in my life in case of emergencies. For example, in months when I don't have any income from the non-profit or the real estate, Ayuuto helps me pay off bills. It's a safety net.

I consider my monthly Ayuuto contribution a bill, like a utility bill or a rent or mortgage payment. It's just one of the bills. If I can afford to put extra money in savings, I do, whether it's $500, or sometimes even $1,000, or even $2000.

When it's my turn and I get the Ayuuto money, I use it for something important, unless I absolutely have to use it to pay monthly bills. I don't want to fritter it away on things that don't last. I try to use it for things that will change my family's life for the better, whether it's buying a car for my child, buying furniture for my office, going on a trip with my children, helping a family member back home, or buying land.

(*I bought some land in Somalia. I put this goal in front of me, and with the practices I've detailed in this book, I finally saved the money to do it. Someday, I want to build a home on the land with my children. I want them to help me build a house there, because it's going to be our vacation home.*)

I also use Ayuuto to buy gold. The only way that I can do so is to buy some when I get my turn. And having gold is like having money in savings. If anything happens, you can resell it. When you don't grow up in a culture that trusts banks, it's often necessary to find other ways to save money. Today I enjoy using the banking and investment system in the U.S. while following other pathways to save money reliably and consistently.

Ayuuto can be a safe money-saving option for many immigrant women, because trusting banks is not something we ever learned in our home countries. Before investing in an Ayuuto circle, it's wise to do extensive research on the Trusted Servant leading each circle, as well as the circle's practices and history.

Some of our Dear Sisters and Somali families may also put their money somewhere in the house under the pillow, under the mattress, or a hidden container. It's important for immigrants to learn that money is safe in a savings account in the U.S. and that you can withdraw your money at any time. Your money can also earn interest through your savings account or other investments, which can help you achieve even more purchasing power for essentials like a home, car, healthcare, or other necessities.

Becoming a homeowner

To become a homeowner, you have to start with a good credit score and a reliable, verifiable source of income that you've had consistently for two years. If you have any money in savings, that will also help you as a borrower.

You will need a downpayment (a lump sum of money) to purchase a home in some cases. There are several programs available that can offer down payment assistance to homebuyers who qualify. Your banker or loan officer can help you look for down payment assistance in your city or county. Find a loan officer at a bank or mortgage company that understands your situation because they'll be aware of the most helpful assistance programs.

There are federal programs and grants for first-time homebuyers that offer practical financial help for down payments and closing costs. Some states offer assistance as well. For example, the state of Minnesota offers a variety of programs for both first-time and repeat homebuyers, plus a refinancing program to lower your mortgage interest rate. Even some of the larger cities like Saint Paul and Minneapolis in Minnesota have their own homebuyer assistance programs.

There are grants, programs and down payment assistance everywhere. You just have to dig in and talk to a good loan officer. Ask them, *"What programs do I qualify for? Can you help me apply?"*

There are requirements for some programs but they're reasonable and actually helpful. For example, in order to apply for some of the down payment assistance options, you have to attend an eight-hour workshop called "Home Stretch" online or in person. You might also have to go for one-on-one financial counseling to gain financial literacy about the money you're receiving.

The workshops and financial educational training are very helpful because if you've never bought or owned a home before, you'll have a lot to learn. Home buying and home ownership are quite different from renting. The information the workshops provide is practical and can save you lots of money and time. The training covers:

- The expenses and responsibilities of home ownership.
- The tax benefits of home ownership.
- The tools and knowledge you must have to buy and successfully own a home.

- Who to call and what to do when you're faced with a home repair (Because you cannot call the landlord to fix it—YOU are now the responsible party.)
- How to take care of your home in winter and summer.

Attending this training is beneficial and educational in helping people transition from being a renter. As a renter, you call the landlord when something breaks and they come and fix it. When you own a home, now *you* are the "landlord."

Here's an example of why this is important. One of my clients bought a home and before he moved in, he had a family emergency in Somalia and left the U.S. It was winter. He didn't turn on the heater and the water pipes froze and broke, and the basement flooded.

It's his home. He just bought it. He didn't take the class. And he didn't realize he needed to either leave the heat on or drain the pipes. (If there is water in your pipes and the weather gets cold enough, the water in the pipes freezes, expands, and can burst the pipe.) The weather in Minnesota is not like back home where it's all the same around the year. This mistake cost him a lot of money.

Learning about homeownership in a new-to-you country is crucial to maintaining a safe and secure home you can enjoy and afford for years.

Four legal documents you must have for financial health

There are four legal documents that will help you safeguard your finances, especially if you pass away, become sick, or can't make decisions for yourself. These documents will also help you assist your older children once they reach the age of 18 and you are not legally able to make health or financial decisions for them.

Wills

What Is a Will?

A will is a legal document that allows you to transfer your property at your death.

A will is a simple way to ensure that your money, property, and personal belongings will be distributed as you wish after your death. A will also allows you to have full use of your property while you are alive. Your will should also appoint an Executor, which is a trustworthy representative that you choose. This person ensures that your property and assets reach the people you designate in your will and that your other wishes are followed.

Does Everyone Need a Will?

The law does not require that you have a will. However, a will is a useful tool that provides you with the ability to control how your estate (your belongings) will be divided. If you die without a will, Minnesota's inheritance laws will control how your estate will be divided. Your property will go to your spouse or closest relatives.

From the Office of Minnesota State Attorney General Keith Ellison, here's a link to tell you more about how your property will be divided if you do not have a will.

https://www.ag.state.mn.us/Consumer/Handbooks/Probate/CH1.asp

Power of Attorney (Medical and Financial)

A power of attorney is a legal document that allows someone else to act on your behalf should you become disabled or incapacitated. A Power of Attorney is a private, inexpensive way to appoint a substitute decision-maker for you, although it may involve help from a lawyer. If you don't create a power of attorney in advance, a friend or family member might have to go to court to have a guardian appointed should you need one. This process can be lengthy and expensive.

You can name both a **financial** power of attorney (for decisions about money and property) and a **medical** power of attorney (for decisions about health care). In Minnesota, the health care document is called a Health Care Directive, or HCD. You'll want to check your state or country's language on which documents address financial and medical guardianship.

Source: U.S> Department of the Interior
https://www.doi.gov/ost/planning-future

Easing your children into adulthood with Power of Attorney

Let's talk about will and trust planning and estate planning. A good friend of mine did not know that in the United States, children are considered adults at age 18. Further, she has no access to their medical information or doctor appointments starting at age 18.

For immigrants in the Somali and East African communities, this fact presents a problem for us. It's very important for my friends as mothers and as immigrants to know what's happening with their children.

My friend's daughter is shy. She's making her way here in America, but still needs her mom's support and guidance. My friend can't do that with her if she cannot access her child's medical and other records. *This is what a Power of Attorney helps my friend to do for and with her daughter until she is old enough and confident enough to act on her own behalf.*

Don't be a victim of poor planning

If you have money in your bank account, if you own properties, if you own lands, and none of your kids are in the paperwork, the state can take those assets if you pass away without a will.

How do you protect your assets? Have a will, and have a power of attorney for yourself and your children so if something happens to you as a parent, you can relax knowing you've chosen someone you trust to make crucial healthcare and financial decisions on your behalf, with your best interests in mind.

A client of mine recently shared a sad story. He was working as a truck driver and his dad was ill. The father wanted to add the son (the truck driver) to his bank account and other important accounts. The truck-driving son kept meaning to make it home at his father's request. Before the visit happened, the truck driver's father passed away.

Because the son had not been added as a Power of Attorney or listed in the will, the son had no claim to his father's records or bank accounts.

As immigrants, we have multiple names and "family" ties that often have no legal record. For example, I have my mom and my brothers and sisters, but I'm not related to them in any way except by blood. I came to America on my own, they came on their own. I have no proof that they're my family.

The truck driver from the story above? He spent three years trying to navigate the "red tape" and paperwork to gain access to his father's estate. I don't even know if he was successful in the end. All of his suffering could have been avoided with a simple will.

A secret in plain sight

Here's another issue we have as Somali and East African immigrant women: **men who have multiple wives.** This practice is not legal in the United States. By law, one human can only legally marry one other human at a time in America.

Somali men who maintain multiple "marriages" may hide their investments, they hide their money from every wife, which is dishonest for the men and harmful for the women and families involved.

Think about it: You have spent all your life with this individual and something happens and you don't know anything about his finances. You don't know how many properties he owns. You don't know where his money is. You don't know what kind of businesses he has. You're in the dark.

That's why, in the Islamic religion, women are encouraged to have their own businesses, income, and investments their husbands cannot touch. Having a will in place can guarantee that your money and possessions will pass to the people you designate, so that your income is *yours.* You can choose to contribute some of all of your income to the household, or keep it for yourself and for emergencies. Islam allows for this freedom for women. Her income is her income. If she chooses to contribute to the household, it's like a charity.

In this way, women can protect themselves from the families of men with multiple wives who may know more than she does about his finances and family obligations. Honorable men will communicate honestly about their multiple families and ensure that their wealth is distributed equally among their children. But, even honorable men wind up leaving their wives to fend for themselves upon their death. Emotions often cloud fairness with jealousy or anger, and family members get left with nothing.

In the United States, there are legal ways, like having these documents in place, to protect yourself from these cultural traditions that can victimize immigrant women and leave them high and dry.

Two ways to protect yourself

1. **Create a will for your estate** (which includes your belongings and assets like property, cars, land, bank accounts, jewelry, artwork, and other important possessions) so that if you die or become incapacitated, you'll know those assets will pass on to the people you choose and trust.
2. **Obtain a Power of Attorney and/or Health Care Directive** for yourself and your children, so that you can still assist your adult children in matters of health care and finances as they grow all up, and so you are secure in someone *you trust* making decisions on your behalf in the event of your serious illness or incapacitation. (Remember that each state has their own requirements.)

We could eliminate so many struggles as immigrants if we take even these two very simple actions. In full transparency, these steps are something I, too, am currently working on as well. I'm with you, my Dear Sisters! It's imperative to make this cultural shift here in the United States. In our countries of origin, family, mothers, fathers, siblings and the women make the decisions, not the government. In America, when you're legally married, your spouse makes your health care and financial decisions if you have a medical emergency or financial incapacitation, unless you specify someone else in your HCD or PA.

Questions to help you begin to legally protect your assets and belongings

1. **Do you have someone you trust to help you or your loved ones if anything happens to you? Who can you trust?**

   ____

   ____

   ____

   ____

2. **Do you have assets/ business or businesses/ homes/ lands here or in other countries?**

   ____

   ____

____

____

3. **Do you know or have an attorney that you can talk to about things?**

____

____

____

____

~~~

My Incredible Sisters, this chapter is a very important chapter to me. As a single parent with multiple businesses, a house, and other valuable assets, I want them all to pass to the people I choose if something happens to me. Planning out these details now means my children continue to have my help and guidance and will have an easier time when I do pass on. It's hard to think about anything happening to you or your children. But you will thank yourself later if (Allah forbid) a tragedy happens and you or someone you love has to respond quickly and wisely. Take care of yourself and your children now, so that you have less to worry about if the worst happens. This is the best thing you can do for yourself and your family, now and always.
~~~

PART II.
CULTIVATE HEALTHY, LOVING RELATIONSHIPS WITH FAMILY

Chapter 10

Cultivate Healthy, Loving Relationships with Your Family

Let me begin this chapter with a warning. Some of you may get upset at the story I'm about to tell. Some of you may believe that family bonds and obligations should always come first and that *you are destined to live a life where you feel worthless.*

Let me tell you more about my father. The truth of the matter is that if it weren't for him I wouldn't be here. He (and my mother) brought me into this world. His responsibility was to provide for me, take care of me, guide me, protect me, show me love, help me to feel important and worthy, and everything else a parent should do for their child.

He chose not to do that. My father left our family when I was a child, built a brand new life with another woman, had babies with her, and never looked back. He chose to create a life for himself apart from his first family. I felt his absence and his abandonment the most when I was struggling in the refugee camp at 13 years old.

We had no food. We had no clothing. The rain was our only wash water. I had devastating mosquito bites on my left leg, which left a huge scar. In fact, I almost lost my leg due to those mosquito bites and the itching, scratching, and infection that followed.

About 20 years later, my father reached out to me again after I moved to America. He asked me to give him money and extra support for him and his other children! It was devastating to me that he could not show up when I was so in need as a child, but now that I had made something of myself, he wanted *me* to show up for *him.*

Healthy relationships begin with your beliefs and your worth

I tell this story to help you understand, My Dear Sister, that this behavior from your family is not okay. You do not have to accept what is not acceptable to you, even if standing up for yourself goes against your culture and what you've been taught to accept from your family. It's not easy to stand up to bullies, especially if they are in your immediate family. But it's possible, as you discover your worth, to create a healthy and loving environment for yourself and your children.

You owe it to yourself and your children to create protection, love, and nourishment around all of you. I'm writing this book because I have four beautiful children. Today, I can give them things my mother could not provide for me or my siblings:

- Love.
- Kindness.
- Communication.
- Connection.
- Affirmation.
- Cuddling.
- Soothing.
- Mentoring.
- Guiding.
- Telling them that I love them.
- Providing emotional support.
- Teaching them right from wrong.
- Teaching them about life.
- Telling them stories.
- Being present when they struggle and triumph.
- Providing an education and an understanding of the world.
- Providing structure in their life.

I didn't know anything about these qualities or skills until I was in my early twenties. From birth to age seven, I was just living in an orchard, wandering around in Somalia. No one really cared for me. I lived with my grandparents until I was seven years old. During that crucial time of development, I was just existing. I had no direction or nurturing…I was completely adrift as a small child.

My mom finally remarried and took us back from her parents. She kept me in the house and taught me how to cook, clean, take care of children, and do laundry. While it was wonderful to have some structure and household education, she didn't talk to me and nurture me or have conversations with me. I felt like I was invisible.

I felt like my mom didn't see me. Like she didn't care for me. She would always demand things or beat me. I don't remember her doing even one loving thing for or with me while I lived with her. I didn't go to school, either, so

I missed out on any sort of education that would teach me how to get ahead in the world—even reading and writing were mysteries!

When the civil war happened in my country, I knew only three things about Somalia (or any other topic):

- The flag was blue with a white star in the middle.
- We had a president named Siad Barre.
- And then sometime in October of that year, there was a big celebration.

Those are the only things I knew about my country at the age of thirteen! I only knew how to do housework and care for children.

As the civil war took hold in Somalia we fled to Djibouti, but my mom still kept me isolated. We settled in the refugee camp and we didn't have anything. I took care of my siblings and did what my mom wanted me to do.

As a young teenager, I lived in the camp until my early 20s under deplorable conditions. We had no shelter and the rain often washed out our belongings. Food was scarce and we had to walk hours to filthy ponds that people and animals would use as a toilet, swimming pool, and bath. We had to boil and filter the water to make it safe to drink every day.

I finally got the chance to leave the camp when a group of church-based women led several groups in getting to other countries. I joined a group headed to the United States.

When I came to North America, my rescuers and the people who helped me were educated middle-class women who wanted to give something back. Many of them (not all) were White and from the west. I learned so many valuable things from them—qualities I had never experienced before. Kindness. Compassion. A willingness to help without any condition. The concept of personal growth. Business ideas, self care, empowerment…and so much more.

For me being an African woman, a Muslim woman, a Somali woman, a young woman who never had experienced kindness—I was amazed that these women came into my life and were so kind and so willing to help.

After I settled in Minneapolis, one of the women who really helped me out during one of my lowest periods was from Haiti. She was a therapist, a doctor. I didn't have money. I couldn't afford her fee. I asked her, *"How can I pay you?"* Instead of paying her with money, she accepted my home cooking in trade for her therapy sessions. I cooked meals and gave them to her.

In exchange, she was willing to guide me and help me heal my inner childhood wounds. She showed me that I deserved much more than what I was getting from my third husband who hit me, bullied me, belittled me, and manipulated me. He said I should feel grateful to be with him because of my minority tribe status. For so long, I felt like a second-class citizen. After working with my therapist, I was able to see the truth of his abuse and believe it for myself. Her help gave me the strength to make plans and leave. What I learned from my journey is that building strong relationships with my family begins with my relationship to myself!

Why do western women seem happier and healthier than Somali women?

I want to talk about something I've noticed. I see a lot of western women in their fifties, sixties, seventies, and even eighties, who are really fit and healthy and feel extremely happy with themselves and their lives. Western women are more valued in US culture because they created that for themselves and stopped taking poor treatment from men. Even though America and other western countries still have a long way to go to achieve complete gender equality, the differences in gender value across cultures are alarming.

My mom and my aunties gave up on life at middle and older age because of our culture's views on women's roles and also how men in our community make them feel. Most women in our culture are expected to take care of everyone and not take time for themselves for crucial activities such as fitness routines or personal creative pursuits.

All of this is made worse by the view of many men in the community who see women primarily as baby-producing machines. Women are forced to get married really young and they have many, many children. By the time that they're in their forties, they stop producing babies because they've been giving birth for decades. My mom had sixteen children. And her mother had sixteen children. And at some point, their bodies got tired and gave up.

Most men in our culture want lots of children. The more children a man has, the more status he has in the community. So, the men we choose as husbands want status in the form of sons who will carry on their name. In our culture (as in many cultures), a woman adds to her *husband's* side of the family. The boys continue the family name, while the family name ends with each girl child.

For my tribe, because I'm a woman, our family name stops with me. But for my brother, his sons will continue the tribe. If a woman has only daughters, she may feel like she's not good enough for not contributing to her husband's family name. Some women may feel worthless for having more girls. Many women don't even know that it's the man's sperm that will determine the gender of the baby! It is assumed that the woman is "at fault" if she gives birth to girls. People will say, *"Oh, she only produces girls."* There's a stigma attached.

Once a wife reaches a certain age, her husband may very well leave her or take on another younger wife who can continue to have babies. One reason that I chose to divorce my third husband, the father of my two youngest children, was because he said, *"You know what? My tribe is small. I want to make sure my tribe gets bigger by having more children. I want a village of children. I'm going to marry younger women to have more babies."*

Some Somali men see having a village of children as an investment in their future. In the United States, the status symbols are money, property, and investments, so that you can live a lifestyle you enjoy and also leave a legacy and lifestyle for your family to enjoy. In our culture, the more babies you have, the more chance you'll have someone to take care of you when you get old.

Because of this core cultural tradition, many women are insecure about their value as human beings and their safety and security as they age. It's hard to cultivate strong, secure family relationships when you are taught to believe you have no value as a person, only as a baby-making machine. This belief is what Somali women must overcome to create real change in our future.

Under this system, women lose in every way. After taking care of everyone—physically, mentally, emotionally—for their entire life, where does that get them? So many Somali women feel betrayed–rightfully so–and become sad and bitter.

The cultural history of devaluing women also affects the way women view and treat each other. Women feel threatened by other women because their worth is measured by their youth and attractiveness and their ability to produce babies.

It's time to stop competing

Sadly, women compete with other women. When we do this, we give men even more power. My Dear Sisters, we can stop this right now. *You don't have to compete with your sister. You're beautiful and unique.* Change begins with us—with women. When we stop competing and start collaborating and supporting each other, our lives change immediately. *You* have so much to offer at every age and stage. You are so much more than your body and your children. First and foremost, *you* are valuable because you are you.

Your worth isn't based on your ability to please men! The truth is in our culture there is no amount of children that will keep a man in a relationship. If he wants to stay in the relationship, if he wants to be a husband, he will stay. Whether you have one child, twenty children, or none.

Healthy families start with strong and valuable women

My dad often calls me when he wants something. It was so hard for me to say no to him because in our culture, no matter what your parents do, they're still your parents and you're obligated to support them at any cost.

I decided to talk to the Imam about this. It was a wake-up call for me to hear the Imam say that I was not obligated to my father. If I chose to help him, it would be considered a charity.

I am obligated to my own children that I brought into this world. As the Imam pointed out, my father brought me into this world and then abandoned me. He chose not to take care of his responsibility. So it's not my responsibility to take care of him. If I choose to help him, it will be a charity. I should only consider this option if I can afford to help him.

Making this shift in my self-worth is what helped make my family relationships stronger, not weaker. When I come from a place of strength and worth with my father, I win, even if at first these changes feel hard for my family members.

Happy memories can help you build healthy relationships

I have such a fondness for one of my sisters. There's a 13 year gap between us, so I felt a lot more like her mother than her sister. I even loved and related to her like her mother.

We enjoyed each other a lot and our relationship felt healthy whenever we spent time together. She often stayed with me on the weekends in my California home years ago. She helped me clean and care for my children, and then I would take her shopping and buy her whatever she wanted. What a dream to be able to give her gifts, time, and teaching!

We loved eating out together and getting into fashion, makeup, and jewelry. I taught her how to cook healthy meals that were fast, efficient, and delicious. Even though my mother did not approve of our close relationship, we stayed loyal and supportive to each other. Because our relationship was so strong and healthy, my sister had the strength to stand up to our mom when she tried to pull us apart.

My sister and I support and care for each other. We love each other. We enjoy spending time together. We can speak honestly about how we feel with each other. If we argue, we make up quickly. Most of all, we value each other and what we each bring to the table. I use this example to help me measure the health and satisfaction of my other relationships. If they don't nourish me in a similar way, I know something has to change.

Boundaries are the key to healthy family bonds

To have a healthy relationship with your family, you must know the kind of family you have. If you know for sure your family is negative and toxic and dysfunctional, you can love them from a distance. You can respect them from a distance.

You can have boundaries–healthy boundaries with your family. (Remember when my mentor Mickey wrote about boundaries several chapters ago? This is a similar concept.) You can teach your family what behaviors and actions are okay or not okay with you, and they need to respect that if they want to spend time with you.

When somebody is extremely toxic, sometimes they don't even know they're toxic. You may think you're crazy when you're around them. They can convince you that *you* are the problem and that *you* must change, when they are not willing to see or change their own issues and negativity.

Dr. Verna Price, author of *Four Kinds of People Who Can Change Your Life,* has taught me love is often assumed in a family. You can love your relatives–your children, your brothers and sisters, your parents, your aunts and uncles. They're your family. There's a reason you were born with them, into them.

When some of your family members make you feel bad, scared, angry, sad, or ashamed, you can still love them. But you can also protect yourself by:

- Respecting them and their human-ness,
- Having your boundaries around your time, your money, and your resources,
- Creating space for you and your own healing and knowing, and
- Distancing yourself from that environment.

When your family members drain you and suck the energy out of you, it's crucial to keep as much of your energy and resources for yourself, while you give them as little time as possible. You may even need to move away from these relatives to escape the pull or the drain on you.

Some family members can belittle you and destroy your dreams and make you feel you're worthless. This behavior may even get worse as you learn to stand up for yourself and set the boundaries that keep you and other loved ones safe. It's crucial to surround yourself with supportive and loving people, either within your family or outside it. You'll need their strength and encouragement as you work on upholding the boundaries you set.

By setting and keeping boundaries, I learned I can love my mother, I can love my siblings, I can respect them as humans. But I needed to change, so that they could no longer hurt me.

For you, this might look like:

- Not having conversations with them every day.
- Calling them or greeting them to see how they're doing, but then keeping the conversation short.

Once they learn that you have boundaries and you're too busy to listen to their trash, they will learn to respect you. I received more respect from my difficult and harmful family members (like my dad and mom) once I practiced these skills.

As for what happened when my dad called to ask me for help for him and his kids? Here's how that story ended:

My father called and said, *"I'm calling to check up on you."*

I knew he wanted something, but he was trying to smooth things over with me first.

He said, *"Are those men, the fathers of your kids, are they supporting you in any way? Are they giving you money? Do they come to visit?"*

I said, "*No, they don't. They don't support us. They don't come and check on them.*
One of them, the younger kid's father, sometimes comes and stays for a couple hours and then leaves."

And my dad said, *"It's okay. I'm sorry to hear that, you know, and they will be fine."*

I said, *"Yes, they will be fine. Just like me. Just like me. They will be fine."*

And for him to hear that from me, he was speechless. And he finally said, "I'm sorry."

I said, *"They will be fine just the way I am fine."*

But I'm not fine. I'm torn inside because I wouldn't have gone through all of the struggles if he was there as a father doing his job. I want to make that clear. The message I have for Somali men is this:

Be a father. Step up. It doesn't matter if you divorce the wife. It doesn't matter if the relationship did not work with the wife. Take responsibility as a man. Take responsibility as a father. Take care of your kids that you brought to this world.

It's as if men have the attitude of "*If I cannot have the woman, I don't care about the kids.*" When Somali men get divorced, they divorce the entire family. That's most Somali men. That's why we have so many kids in jails and on drugs and on the streets, and six feet underground. It's terrifying. Hennepin County Jail is full of Somali kids. Last year alone, we lost over 20 local Somali kids due to drugs and shootings and drug overdoses.

Where are the fathers? You go to Starbucks, they're full of Somali men. You go to some restaurants, they're full of Somali men. You go to the Somali mall, they're full of Somali men.
You go out on lakes, they're full of Somali guys. At school conferences, there are almost *no* Somali fathers taking part.

There is taboo about speaking on this matter in our communities, and we need to have the conversation. Children need their fathers. I needed my father. Fathers need to step up and take responsibility for raising their children–*all of their children.*

How to start setting boundaries with your family

- Be clear in your own mind about the behavior you will and won't accept from family members. What you will accept from your ex husband will be different from what you'll accept from your mom.
- The next time someone crosses your boundary, inform them of your choice. For example, I do not take calls after 9pm. I don't answer my phone after this time. If someone tries to call me or leave me a message, I contact them the next day and inform them that I don't answer my phone after 9pm.
- Follow through on what you say you will do if someone violates your boundary. For example, some people I know like to gossip on the phone. If they go down that road when we speak, I will change the subject and let them know I do not talk about other people in harmful ways. I also tell them what is okay to talk about–their goals, family, work, or desires–something we can both benefit from.

Questions to help you improve your family relationships

1. **Do you have a healthy relationship with your family? Yes/ No**

____

____

____

____

____

____

2. How does it feel to have a healthy relationship with the people you love?

____

____

____

____

____

____

3. What boundaries do you have with the people in your life?

____

____

____

____

____

____

____

~~~

My Dear Brave Sisters, believe me when I tell you that it was not easy for me to write this chapter because it was not easy to create boundaries with people that supposedly love you and protect you and now you have to protect yourself from them. It is very lonely and scary to distance yourself from unhealthy people and create a healthy environment for yourself and for the people you love. But it is doable and it is worth the hard work and the loneliness you go through while creating it. Life with boundaries is peaceful, joyful, stable, and safe.
~~~

Chapter 11

Parenting Well

As Somali parents, we have the power to break destructive cycles of hardship, abuse, struggle, and power imbalances in our families. Change first begins within us as individuals, as we talked about in the last chapter. Those changes continue to grow and flourish when making changes in our parenting.

In our culture, large families are the norm. Moms can feel exhausted, overwhelmed, and even hopeless about managing so many children, and with good reason! Parenting is hard work. Children need so much care and attention to grow up well and be healthy, strong, and smart.

Observations on child spacing

I'm here to tell you that it's **okay for you to consider how many children you want to have as you plan your family.** It's okay to have fewer children—only as many as you can support well with your time, energy, and financial resources. This is a new concept in our culture. Some Somali women are only just beginning to understand that they have choices about how big their family is, how far apart to space their children, and what steps to take to make those choices a reality.

The Quran provides even stronger evidence of these choices:

"The Quran does not prohibit birth control, nor does it forbid a husband or wife to space pregnancies or limit their number.

The Quran says: "The mothers shall give suck to their offspring for two whole years."

According to Islamic teachings, Allah encourages women to space childbirth primarily to protect the health of both the mother and child. The Quran emphasizes the importance of providing proper care and nourishment to children, and breastfeeding is seen as a natural form of birth control that benefits both parties; this aligns with the understanding that a mother needs time to recover physically and emotionally between pregnancies to adequately care for her children."

"Key points to consider:

Health benefits:
The Quran mentions the importance of breastfeeding, which naturally spaces births and is considered beneficial for the baby's health and development.

No burdening oneself:
Islamic scholars interpret verses in the Quran to mean that Allah does not want to burden believers with excessive childbearing, implying that responsible family planning is encouraged.

Quality over quantity:
The focus is on raising healthy and well-cared for children rather than having a large family without proper provision."

The hardest job in the world is to be a single parent because you have to be everything to this little child or the children you brought to this world. The job is endless, you have to be equipped and you have to create resources and a community to help you raise them well.

As a single parent, you are the world to your children. You are the mom, you cook, you clean the house, you do the laundry, you work, you go shopping, you are the doctor, you are the nurse, you are the teacher, you pay the bills, you take them to Dugsi (Islamic studies), you are the emotional support, you are the provider, you are the protector, you are the friend, the mentor and the advisor. You are more than a mom, you are priceless.

When women feel empowered in their families, the whole family improves. The children get better care from mothers who have energy, education, and experience to share with love, not from mothers who are exhausted, overwhelmed, or just surviving.

Observations on parenting

Because my family made me the "black sheep" of our household from a very early age, I grew up as an observer—often feeling separate and forgotten by my family. I've shared many stories from my life to illustrate this perspective–and observation has been one of the greatest gifts for me. Being able to see what's really going on is the first step to creating lasting change.

Even when I'm in a community or business meeting, I observe and evaluate the whole situation, how people are acting, what they're saying, what emotions and behaviors are at the surface.

Because I can observe well, I know the places in my life that are satisfying and good, as well as the areas I want to change and grow. I have the power to change my life and make it better, and so do you, my Dear Sister!

Here's what I observe about parenting in our culture. I want to shine a light on it not to judge my Dear Sisters, but to help us all work for change that makes better lives for everyone—especially the Somali women I love and care about so deeply.

A lot of the parenting I see in my community looks like:

- Children fearing their mother being angry, overwhelmed, and exhausted.
- Mothers who don't have loving and connected relationships with their children, even though their intentions are good.
- Adults screaming and yelling at their children.
- Adults saying "How dare you?" and "Why did you do that?" to their children, or even "What's wrong with you?"

Here's what I *would like* to observe about our Somali parenting community:

- Mothers empowering their children to be strong, to have minds of their own.
- Mothers stopping to see their childrens' souls and hearts.
- Mothers understanding that their kids can feel and sense if their mother is angry.

Our job is to protect our children. If we don't heal and change the way we do things with our children, then we're raising children who don't know how to deal with hard times or reach for better lives for themselves. We brought our children to this world. And as parents, it's our job to protect them and teach them how to protect themselves.

Change begins with ourselves and how we parent. If we could change the way we collectively parent, we would not have broken homes, we would not have broken kids, we would not have women who are struggling mentally, physically, and emotionally. We would all enjoy more happiness and ease and comfort in our families.

Healthy boundaries, building a relationship, trusting others

As a single mother who survived so much emotional, sexual, and physical abuse in my family, I advise other mothers to be very careful about who you trust with your children. I don't care if they're family members. I don't care if they're friends or neighbors. You have to make sure the people who watch and care for your kids are mentally healthy and stable. Also, *you* have to know and talk to your kids about who to trust and who not to trust.

Talk to your kids. Tell them that their body is their body. Nobody is allowed to touch it. Let them know it's okay for them to tell you if someone touches them. Help them understand what healthy, safe touch looks and feels like, and when and how to speak up about their bodies and who touches them. Make sure that you have healthy communication. The best thing that you could do for your kids is to listen and tell them that no matter what happens and whatever they go through, they can come to you and talk about it.

As parents, even when we discipline them, we need to show our kids examples of safe and loving touch. *It's not necessary to hit your children to get them to behave.*

Children need to learn by our example the difference between loving, safe, familiar touch that feels good in their souls, and touch that victimizes them and feels bad all over, even if the *attention* they receive might feel good for a short time.

Build a relationship with your child as early as possible to guide them. Let them know *"I'm here to help you, guide you, support you, and uplift you. Whatever happens, we can solve it together."*

As a parent, you can teach your children to lead themselves instead of following along in tough situations. You can teach them about their private parts and what to watch out for if someone touches them or wants to touch them. They get to decide what feels good and safe in their bodies when they are around friends and loved ones. When you talk openly and honestly and frequently to your kids, it lets them know they can tell you anything and not be afraid. You won't judge them. You will listen to them and they will feel safe.

If your child doesn't feel safe with you, what do you think will happen to them? They will seek affirmation from somewhere else. They will do things that you're not happy with. They will hide things from you.

My kids trust me and I trust them, so they tell me everything, everything. Even when they misbehave, they tell me about it. We discuss what happened in a calm and loving way. I ask them what they learned from the situations they get into. Sometimes there are consequences for their behavior—and I get them involved in deciding what those consequences should be. I send them away for a short time to think about what's fair—how they should change their behavior. It's always a discussion, never an angry screaming match.

It took me a long time to learn how to do this, because I didn't grow up with healthy parenting examples. I had to learn how to stay calm when my kids shared something hard with me. I had to let my anger and fear wash over me and not come out onto them. But now, my kids and I have a strong and loving relationship we all enjoy.

Empowering your kids to think freely

One of the women I mentor has a 16 year old daughter. This teenager was born in the United States, but is a Somali Muslim child. The girl came to her mother and mentioned she had started dating a boy her age.

A typical Somali mother would scream and yell and say *"Haram, against the religion! What's wrong with you?"* and on and on.

But this mother tried something different. She asked what the boy was like. And what her teen liked about him. And whether she thought the relationship was appropriate or not. They dove into what their religion and culture advised about such relationships. In the end, it may not matter so much whether the girl continued to date this boy. The triumph was that the mother and daughter could discuss the whole thing openly and without shame or anger.

As a mother, you want your children to be safe, happy, and taken care of. It's also crucial to SHOW your children how to get those things for themselves. Open communication and giving your children the freedom to think through these life events on their own is what moves us forward as healthy families, breaking the chains of so much trauma that so many of us have endured. You can do things differently.

Your children will surprise you

I know another mom who accompanied her high school daughter to school on "meet the teacher" day. She took the time to meet all her daughter's teachers and to tell them about what kind of child her daughter is. What to expect from her. This mom met the principal and explored the school itself.

And yet, this teenager just did not like school. As she moved through school, she only wanted to hang out with her friends. She fell behind in her classes and her grades dropped down so low she was at risk of not graduating with her friends. Even after changing schools four times in four years, school was still a huge struggle for this young girl.

This girl's mom nearly gave up on her in March of her senior year. Finally, the mom had a serious conversation with her daughter. "I'm done," the mom said. "First of all, you're not going to school and graduating for me. It's *your* life. Do whatever you want."

Her teacher said *"I'm so sorry, but you won't be able to graduate."*

It was the message she needed to make a big change. All of a sudden, a switch flipped inside her and she decided to try harder. This teenager studied night and day, weekends and evenings to catch up. She finally graduated, all on her own! It hit her that she wouldn't graduate with her school and peers and she'd have to deal with what people would think of her. That made her turn around like you wouldn't believe.

When we treat our kids like respected humans and give them the ability to choose and decide their lives (with help and guidance, but without shame and screaming), they gain strength and the self-worth it takes to power through hard events and crucial milestones.

Spending time with your children is key

Finding ways to spend quality time with your kids can help them build the behaviors you want them to have.

But, how do you spend time with them when finances are tight and you have a large family? Here in Minnesota, there are a surprising number of places and activities your family can enjoy for *free:*

- The Minnesota Zoo (if you have a medical assistance card)
- Como Park Zoo
- The Minneapolis Institute of Art
- The Walker Art Museum (once-per-month free family nights–check their website calendar)

- Parks, lakes, rivers, and creeks–having a barbeque or picnic at the parks or lakes.
- Tuesday night movies at some theaters (reduced ticket and snack prices)

It's also fun and enriching to cook, read (especially about Islam!), or watch a show with your kids. And your kids benefit from your attention! It's not so important what you choose, as long as you're present and engaged with them. Spending time with your children creates trust with them—so that they feel safe and comfortable sharing anything with you.

Which brings me back to you and making sure you are getting enough sleep, taking care of your health, and prioritizing yourself from time to time as well–so that you can show up well for your kids. Some of the help you need around the house can and should come from your older children. Doing chores together is another way to spend time with your children, plus they learn the skills they'll need when they move into their own homes later in life.

If you have older children and begin to make some of these changes, you might get some resistance from them at first, because everyone struggles with change. But keep at it. Be consistent. Make little changes each week or month in the way you show up for your children. You will see results if you keep going.

Even though I often struggle to find balance between working and providing for my children and spending time with them, what I'm most proud of is the safe space at work I've created for them and me. Five days a week, they do their homework and we eat meals at my office. We fold in what has to be done as a family–it works for us. You get to discover and integrate what works for you and your family.

My Dear Sister, parenting is hard work. It never ends. It's relentless at times. Your kids will make mistakes. You will make mistakes. They won't act how you want them to act all the time. They will fight, argue, and make choices you don't want them to make. You will lose your temper sometimes.

And still, our job is to give them firm boundaries and a soft place to call home where they know they are cared for and loved and valued—without rage or shame. Where they know what's allowed and what is not. If you can do that most of the time, you'll win. You'll change your family story.

Here is the behavior that is NOT allowed in our home:

- Lying.
- Stealing.
- Hurting others.
- Cussing.

I set these boundaries in my home to teach them to recognize these harmful behaviors in others. My kids need to understand that there are good people, bad people, ugly people, liars, and manipulators in the world. I help them understand how to be aware and alert about the difference and watch out for the manipulators and the liars and the signs of them—just as much as they can recognize the signs of safety and friendship in others. I also made my children learn the Quran. I want them to go to the Quran as a loving resource for education about life and how to value themselves and others and have a healthy relationship with Allah.

It wasn't easy for me to raise healthy, beautiful, successful kids. I worked so hard to protect them, to guide them, to love them, to protect their ears, their heart, their soul, their mind. As a parent, you go to school, school conferences. You work all day and you're exhausted and you have to go to the school conference and make sure your kids are learning or see where they are struggling. You have to monitor what's happening in your kids' lives, even when you're not always there. It wasn't easy for me to make sure other kids, some men, or so-called teachers were not beating up my children.

The answer is to never give up on the child. Just like that mom whose daughter almost did not graduate. That mom saw that her daughter needed to choose the right path for herself, but she never gave up on her daughter.

Even when your kids test your very last ounce of patience, don't give up on them. Give them the lessons they need to make good choices. Like another mom I know whose daughter couldn't wait to leave the house and get out on her own:

"I remember my daughter telling me that she can't wait to leave when she's 18, she can't wait to be 18 so she can leave. At that time she was 16.

I said, 'Why are you waiting until 18? That's a whole year. You don't want to suffer.
If you feel like you're suffocating and you're suffering, you don't have to wait until you're 18.'

"I said, 'I'm going to do you a favor and let you leave with the clothes that you have on and the rest of the stuff, they're mine. The phone is mine. I'm paying for it. The clothes are mine. I'm paying for them. All of the shoes you're wearing, they're mine. I paid for them. The jewelry you're wearing and the makeup you have, they're mine. I paid for them. It's your choice. You can leave. Just leave with the clothes on.'

That gave her a different perspective. She was shocked. She was surprised. 'None of this stuff is mine?'

I'm the mom putting a roof over your head. I am buying things. As a young Somali woman, you can't wear makeup. You can't have nail polish. You can't have lipstick. But she was my only girl at that time, so I allowed it. I bought her lipstick. I bought her nail polish. I bought her beautiful clothes and dresses. It was her choice to share it with her friends.

And now, after those crucial conversations, she's 20 and she's not going anywhere.

She sees her peers, her friends, suffering and being controlled.

I said to her, 'You know what? Be kind. Be a leader, not a follower. Listen. You do not need to believe everything that anyone says to you. You have to do your own research. Question things.
If somebody asks you a favor, don't say yes. Tell them, 'Let me think about it.' And sleep on it.'"

This mom changed the way she parented—and her kids changed too! She is raising her daughter to have freedom, to think wisely for herself, to make good decisions after careful thought and research.

When you raise your children this way, the results can really surprise you. This same mom came to me a few years later to finish her story: .

"They're in college. My daughter has a clothing store. My son is working on his mortgage license. They both have cars. They have business of their own.

It wasn't easy. The other weekend when I was busy for several days at a training summit, my son and daughter were in the office making phone calls, filling out paperwork with clients.

The door was open, my business was running, because they were all in here doing their business. They were working, working, working, and talking to clients. I called during my breaks, and checked in...I had tears in my eyes. My heart was full. I did that.

I was so proud of them and me. At that age, being young, I did that. They have a credit score of 800. They have better credit than me! I made sure by the time they were 18, their score was up that high.

I am a living legacy—not just because of how I raised my children, but because I'm a responsible human being with a humble heart, a belief that I can be a leader, that I can take care of the people I love, and that we have loving relationships that support each other well.

I built my business so they could thrive. I'm teaching them to give back to their community by mentoring the young men and women around them.

When we raise our children to be loving leaders, our whole community wins. When we teach them to give back, not be selfish, and share their knowledge with others—THAT is the true legacy I want to leave not only my children, but everyone I touch and everyone THEY touch."

How to change the way you parent

- Start by becoming the observer. Notice how you respond and react to your children when they misbehave. Notice your anger or fear. Notice how you interact with your children each day and how much time you spend together.
- Make a plan to do one activity together this week as a family, even if it is just a walk to the park for some playtime or a picnic. Leave the screens at home. Talk to each other.
- Notice what everyone's response is to your activity together. Did it feel boring? Fun? Difficult?
- Be willing to keep spending time together consistently–even if it's uncomfortable at first. You don't have to make sure everyone gets along or has a good time. It's enough to reserve the time together at first. It will take your family time to start enjoying and anticipating "new" ways to be together.

Questions to help you observe and enhance your parenting

1. **How do you feel about your parenting style if you have a child/ children?**

____

____

____

____

2. **What are the things that happened to you as a kid that you don't want your children to go through?**

____

____

____

____

____

____

3. **What are your plans to have healthy and loving relationships with your children?**

____

____

____

____

____

____

~~~
~~~

My Dear Hardworking Sisters, I am beyond grateful to Allah for giving me four precious children. I honor and pray to Allah to guide us with this journey of parenting. I am a true witness to the amazing hard work we are doing as parents and I would not exchange it for anything else. I encourage you to seek help when you need to and create a healthy, supportive environment, resources, and community that you trust. It takes a whole village to raise children that are mentally stable and successful.

Chapter 12

Dating Well

So many Somali Women in their 40s, 50s, and beyond are sad, alone, scared, or angry, because of how our culture encourages men to treat them. If we reach the end of our reproductive years, cannot have children, or birth only girls, or never marry, our value only goes down in the eyes of many Somali and other men.

My enjoyment of life started in my 40s. At this age, I've become fully aware of who I am, what I want, and what I need. I am wiser, I know my body well, and I am confident. I birthed and raised all my children, and now I can enjoy living for myself.

My Dear Sister, love yourself enough to attract the partner you need and want to enjoy life with. Now it is time to plan what you want in life: traveling, starting a business, writing, taking trips on the weekend, and loving your life.

Please know, My Dear Sisters, that I speak from the voice of observation and experience. I love you, care for you, and I'm not putting down my culture, religion, or YOU. *The way we are being treated for generations in relationships by men is unacceptable.* I've seen it with my mother, my aunties, my community, and my friends. We don't know our own value or the value of a healthy foundation. We need to be respected, loved, and revered by our men. We need to *teach* them how to treat us, because they have never learned how to do it in their families. It may be painful and sad to hear the truth. It's time to change our experience. And it has to start with us, My Dear Sisters.

One way to begin to make those changes is to get clear on what you want from dating. To think about your value and what you bring to a relationship apart from having babies (and be assured, you bring a lot of value just by being you, Dear Sister.)

Something I'm creating for myself right now is having a healthy relationship with a husband and a partner. It's crucial to me to have boundaries in a relationship and to have a partner who is loving and kind and also sees me as valuable beyond my baby-producing ability. I'm trying to create a healthy partnership like the ones I see in Western culture and that I also learned from our religion. We hold hands, go to parks, eat together, have barbecues, and build a healthy relationship where we have deep, fruitful conversations.

When I think about my future husband, those are the things that I am envisioning with him so that we can create memories together. I also imagine traveling, going to picnics, going walking, watching movies, praying, going to the mosque, creating art or meals together, having soulful conversations about life, watching our kids grow, and having grandkids.

I'll be 50 years old soon, and I know this life is possible, even though there are so many young women around me who may seem more enticing to the men in my community.

I don't want to be sitting at home and tired. There are so many Somali women in their 50s and 60s that have diabetes, high cholesterol, high blood pressure, joint aches, and can't sleep well. Some of these women are dragging, depressed, sad, bitter, angry with the world. I don't want to be that. I've seen it with my grandmother on my dad's side of the family. I've seen it with my own mother and my auntie, and I don't want that.

I took a risk and started living my life so differently here in the United States. I've reached for what I wanted for myself and for my kids. I've worked hard to make changes in my life and grow out of the control that so many Somali women face in our culture. I know it's possible to have the healthy relationship I want. I know it's possible to grow old and be happy and excited about life while I enjoy traveling and taking care of my mental, physical, and emotional health.

What happened to the vision of two people falling in love, having a family, watching their kids grow and get married, watching their kids have kids, families coming together to enjoy milestones, celebrations, and religious holidays? I want that, and that's something I'm creating for my kids.

I put it in my heart and in my core and even on paper! I talk to the guy that I'm dating.

"Listen, when are you ready to step up to my plate and my world? You're going to buy me a seven-bedroom, five-bathroom, three-living room house with a huge kitchen and huge backyard, because I'm going to have my grandkids come over."

I tell him, *"My daughter-in-law, my son-in-law come over, my kids, your kids and their kids come over at least twice a year and have a party, a family gathering, and we enjoy ourselves."*

Many men and women in our culture don't even think to ask themselves important questions about what they want. What their purpose is. What their dreams are. Even the man I'm dating hadn't ever given it much thought.

Shortly after I began seeing him, I brought up a discussion:

"I want to bring families together and have an education. I want to have retreats in my home where I invite women and invite families and get together and socialize and also learn because I want to teach women. It's possible. I don't care how old you are. It's possible to be happy. It's possible to have a beautiful life. It's possible to create your dream life. As long as you're breathing and alive, the dream is endless."

I said to this man, *"What is your dream? Enrich your dream. What is your legacy? What is your purpose in this world? Why do you think you're here?"*

He said, *"Those are great questions. I don't know."*

He's still thinking about it. It never even occurs to many people to ask themselves these questions. When you're struggling to survive or living in an abusive relationship, it's hard to think very far into the future. And still, we must ask these questions to be able to change the way we live.

I told this man that I need him to have a plan for the next 5 and 10 years. I want to see his goals and plans for himself and with me. He's been working on that while I have a clear plan of what I want to do.

I told him in that plan of our house, *"You're going to have an office on one side and I'm going to have an office on one side and we're going to work to empower the world. Because you are a father, you are a man, and you are a Somali man, you need to step up and do something about the crisis that we're going through."* It is up to him to step up, but my role will be to encourage and support him if he chooses.

Loving ourselves before falling in love

The most important thing that I want to tell single women and single mothers about dating is whether you have two, three, five, more, or no children, you must love yourself first! We need to validate ourselves and discover how we can be complete and content with ourselves before getting romantically involved with a man.

There *are* good men out there. We don't have to settle for less. We don't have to give in to pressure. A lot of men will pressure women to get married quickly. A lot of us who follow the Muslim faith (women *and* men) don't want to date, because it's against our religion to date.

I know it's against our religion, but we've got to know this person we're planning to spend our life with! We've got to know that he is trustworthy and honest and that we (and our children, for those that have children) are safe.

We're no longer young and naive. As grown women, our parents are not going to be involved, making sure we're marrying the right person. We're adults, we have kids we need to keep safe, we have responsibilities and those are the most important things. It's responsible and reasonable and smart to get to know a potential life partner—for three months, six months, one year—however long it takes!

I have a list I created. First, I don't want to be with a married man. But I do want a man who has been married before and is divorced and on his own now. I want a man who is a father and knows how to be a father and takes responsibility for his children. I want a man who has a stable job and a strong work ethic.

I want a man who is patient and faithful to one woman only. A man I can retire with. I don't believe in multiple marriages. I want a man who has a relationship with God, and who loves kids. I want a man who can carry his end of a conversation and is not so into himself he cannot see who I am or meet my needs.

There are smart, educated, and respectful men out there! Don't settle for less because they want to get married. You don't have to give in and say, *"I want a halal marriage, I want a partner"*.

Tips for Dating Safely

Safe dating practices are essential for making your relationship vision come to life. Here are several simple tips you'll remember easily.

1. Meet a new person in a neutral place that is not your home. Meet up for coffee or a meal. Go for a walk in the park or around a lake. Wait to allow a new person into your home and around your children (if you have kids.)

2. Understand your dating partner's character before you invite them to get to know you more deeply. Consider talking to friends and family in the community to find out more about this person's values and character. Make sure they match your own.

3. Know what you're looking for. Be picky. Know your value. Date only men who understand that you have value just for who you are.

4. Take it slowly. Allow a friendship to grow before romance, even though it can be hard to slow down sometimes. There is no rush to get married, no matter what anyone tells you. You must be sure this person is safe and that you can like or love them for years before you take that step.

5. Wait to introduce your children to your dating partner for several months until you know where the relationship is going and that you feel they are safe for your kids to be around.

6. Create a network of "babysitters" in your neighborhood so that you can have a safe person watch your children while you're on a date with a new person. Return the favor to your Sister who also wants to date!

7. Take time between relationships or marriages to heal from the last one.

8. Look for other ways to heal your loneliness or isolation outside of dating relationships (because when you are lonely and isolated, you are more vulnerable to the agendas of men who don't really care about you.)

There are so many wounded and mentally ill men out there, unfortunately. They look normal, they dress normal, and they talk normal so you think they are healthy, but they are sick. They are often depressed, wounded, angry, sad, and so much more. Men who don't take care of themselves are also a concern. Watch out for those who do drugs, smoke hookah, drink alcohol and chew khat (greet leaves.)

There are some so-called religious men who manipulate women into marriage because they want halal marriage. They believe that women should have a partner and shouldn't be alone. Most of those men have multiple wives, but they don't treat them fairly or equally according to their religion.. They can't provide for them and their kids so those women and children struggle in the system.

There are other heartless, immoral. men with huge egos that think women are toys. They play with women's emotions, their hearts, their minds, and manipulate them. Those men are often businessmen, who offer those vulnerable women money to be their secret wives so they can sleep with them. These men take women to hotels on the weekends or rent an apartment in the city.

Some of those men hide or deny that they have been married or have children or multiple wives and children. My second ex-husband did this very thing. He hid and denied some of his children and ex-wives. We have to be extremely cautious and 10 steps ahead of these toxic men. You have to cut the cord of thinking that you are not complete if you don't have a man in your life.

My Dear Sister, I want you to know what you deserve and what you want. I want you to love yourself, to respect yourself, and to prioritize yourself. Once you know your value, your wants, and your needs, you can finally carry yourself with dignity. The right man who deserves you will come to you. Don't ever ever settle for less. You are the dream of every man and you have to believe that. If you don't believe it, let's work on it together. **Be the woman every man wants by knowing exactly who you are and being authentically *you* every single day.**

What can happen when you don't date safely

Bad things often happen to good women in our community. A woman I know had to leave the state to protect herself from a dating relationship gone bad. Her dating partner kept coming to her house. He physically beat her and her daughter. He had a mental illness that made him unsafe to handle in a relationship.

Single moms are even more vulnerable to bad dating partners, so it's extra important to be exceptionally careful when starting to date.

What to watch out for in your dating partner

When you begin to date in your community, it's imperative to watch out for any "red flags" that may come up in the man you date. Here are some common ones:

1. **Pressure to see your home or your children too soon.** *A man my friend dated wanted to see her house and family only two weeks after they met. She didn't feel comfortable allowing him into her family or home before she knew him better. He suspected her of lying and hiding something from him–like being married. He stopped dating her because of this suspicion. She was sad initially because she thought he was a good guy, but ultimately she had to go with her gut and do what felt right to her. They stopped seeing each other. Later on, he approached my friend again after seeing how successful she had become in the community. But, the fact that he didn't trust her at first was enough for her to turn down his next advance.*

   His argument was that if he was going to consider marriage with my friend, he had a aright to know where she lived and to know her family. But really, it's HER decision when to allow a man to meet her family or see her home.

2. **Calling you too late at night.** If a man calls you after 9 in the evening, his intentions may not be the best. And, if you're lonely and isolated, you can feel extra vulnerable later in the evening and may make a bad decision around meeting someone who you don't know is safe. Many men know how to manipulate vulnerable women. A man once called another woman I know after 9 and said,

   "You're tired, you need somebody to massage your feet. You probably need your shoulders rubbed, you know, give you a back massage... you're a single mom– you need somebody who can help you and make tea for you, rub your back and make your dinner so you can watch a movie and relax!"

   Every woman wants to hear these words! But, don't settle. Instead of getting to know you properly, he's trying to be romantic with you and get you to fall for him!

3. **Being sexually explicit with you.** Here's another short story from a woman in my community:

   "One evening, I was rocking my son to sleep when my phone rang. I picked it up (my first mistake) and he asked "Are you in bed? What clothes are you wearing?"

   I've experienced other overtly sexual behaviors from men, like:
   - Undressing me with their eyes
   - The creepy once-over that some men give you on the street
   - Compliments that are too sexual
   - Flicking their tongue at me in a suggestive way

4. **Social media scam artists** There are many men that try to reach out and target women on social media. These random messages can seem friendly and admiring at first, but don't engage. These men are really good at what they do, and they know just the right words to hook you into their scheme. There is always a scam at the end of the conversation —usually for money. Learn to see these messages for what they are. You don't need to respond in moments of loneliness. Remember your worth. A true partner will get to know you in ways that feel safe and honest.

These behaviors tell you a lot about a man. When a man behaves this way with you, it's time to leave, hang up the phone, or connect with friends who value you. Notice how a man talks with you. How he holds himself. Whether he's willing to answer legitimate questions about who he is, where he works, what his goals are, how he views relationships. Whether he's been married before or has children. How many? Where are they located? How does he support them?

The men you meet may not like having to be this accountable. They often just want to say the "right" thing to get you to like them—so their lives can continue just as they are. Asking for change is uncomfortable and necessary. You are worth honesty, integrity, and being valued by your partner. Let yourself get used to the belief that any man would be privileged to know you, date you, or marry you one day. They must measure up to your standards to have that kind of access to you and your family.

There are many stories of men who don't really value women in our community:

"The man I had dated briefly 6 years ago reached out after he saw me on TV and after I got my college bachelor's degree. He left me because I wouldn't let him see my house or meet my children right away. He said he made a mistake letting me go all those years ago, and could he try to fix that and start over? Sadly for him, I had moved on and was dating someone new. When this man left me years ago, I chose to believe in myself and my own worth. Turns out he was not the only option for me. I learned I could choose the type of men I date—and let them go if they don't fit my goals and visions for myself and my safety."

So can you, Dear Sister!

When women value themselves, men can feel it and smell it and taste it. Men who are looking for "easy targets" to manipulate and control know they can't mess with us when we value ourselves. So they move on. Dear Sister, when you hold yourself with dignity and value, you will begin to attract different kinds of men into your life. Keep going with your learning and changing, even when it feels impossible. All the small changes you make now will pay off for you in big and small ways soon.

Valuable men who have integrity and honor and honesty want women who have the same qualities. It's time to cultivate those qualities—your boundaries and limits—to have the life and partner you really want.

The man I'm with today is:

- A good listener
- A good talker—we can talk for hours and hours together
- Drug-free, smoke-free, and alcohol-free
- Supportive in all the ways (emotionally, mentally, and empowers me to reach all my dreams)

What you can do today to date well

My Dear Sister, making changes in the way you date and relate with men can be hard and lonely at first. You'll be so tempted to go back to your old habits when you feel isolated, overwhelmed with your children, or alone.

Here's what worked for me to get through this phase:

- Stay off of social media and don't answer your phone after 9pm. (This is when I was most vulnerable to creepy, manipulative men who would tell me what I wanted to hear to get what they wanted from me.)
- Be open to working on yourself—read new self-help books, take some classes, or learn how to manage your finances and even save and invest money!
- Share babysitting/child-watch responsibilities with women in your community, so you can all get the time you need to work on yourselves.
- Journal after the kids are in bed—write out your feelings and your dreams and goals. Imagine the life you want and write it down!
- Talk to supportive, healthy friends and family who won't judge you.
- Work on how you parent your children and connect more deeply with them.
- Listen to growth-minded podcasts or audiobooks while you do the dishes, clean the house, or ride in the car. (See my list of recommendations at the end of the book.)
- When a relationship gets serious, go to premarital counseling before getting married to make sure you are compatible and the relationship has a chance to last.

How to change your loneliness and isolation

Many women in our culture are stuck in a loneliness cycle. It's hard– almost impossible– to make friends with other women, because we always believe we have to compete with each other. Most men are not safe to interact with and do not know how to be friends with women without trying to date or have sex with us. Even our family relationships are not always safe! So, how do we come together and feel like a true community of valuable women (who date and marry partners who respect them?)

If we want partners who will meet our needs and support us while we support and care for them, we have to begin with ourselves! I knew I was going to create a beautiful life and I have. I'm ready to add to that life with a stable marriage to a good man. I know in my heart there is a beautiful man out there who is meant for me. I don't know if he is the man I am talking to now, when or where I'll meet him, but I am confident that it will happen.

I've been dating a man for the last three years and he is everything that I want in a man. But sometimes we're not patient. We want things really quickly. I wasn't patient. But this man is patient with me.

I said, *"I want to have a healthy marriage. I want us to grow together. I want a stable relationship. And if you're not ready for me and what I need, then I don't want anything to do with you."*

And he said, *"Well, if you want to be with me, give us a chance. You know, let me get to know you and you get to know me because you've been married before and I've been married too. Marriage is not easy and we need to do it right this time."*

He said, "*we like somebody; then we get really excited. So we get married and we find out that we're not compatible with that person. How does that serve us?"*

That was hard for me to hear, but necessary. Why do we have so many marriages? In our (East African) culture, we're not supposed to date. We don't date. A man comes and talks to you for a few weeks, but there is somebody mediating the meetings. It's based on religion, not culture. So, if a man likes a woman, he will ask her parents. Introductions are made through friends or someone in the community. No wonder so many marriages fall apart when each partner barely knows the other!

As we make changes within ourselves, we must be patient with seeing and talking with the men we date, and we must be patient with ourselves. Time will tell you about people, and reveal their true colors. We must make safe decisions about whom to date for ourselves and for our children. When we practice these new beliefs and behaviors, women can be empowered to create the relationships that satisfy them, keep their children safe, and never question their value again!

Questions to help you date safely

1. **What are you looking for in a partner?**

____

____

____

____

____

____

2. Do you have a list of qualities you want in a partner? What are they?

____

____

____

____

____

____

____

____

3. Do you have a list of boundaries that you won't compromise? What are they?

____

____

____

____

____

____

____

____

~~~

My Gorgeous Sisters, in this chapter, I had to really think about our women, mothers, aunties, grandmothers, our sisters, nieces and our daughters. The amount of abuse I have seen, witnessed, heard, and been through by men in our community is unacceptable. I will not let my precious daughters, nieces and sisters be hurt anymore. You are the reason I am writing this book, my Courageous Sister. You are the one who can benefit from this book if you are ready for it and you can make positive changes permanently for yourself and your loved ones. It all happens one day, one small choice at a time. You've got this!
~~~

Chapter 13

How to Get Out of a Toxic Relationship

I was nine months pregnant when I told my second husband I wanted a divorce.

I was going to be induced the following day and we were homeless because my husband chose not to provide for us. Being nine months pregnant, I couldn't get a job either. I was staying with my cousin's friend, who was helping me.

I said to my husband, *"Can we go for a walk and talk?"*

While walking with him, side by side, I said, *"This is not working. You're not being responsible. And I don't want to be in this situation. So let's get divorced."*

He stopped, turned, and stepped in front of me. He put his arms around my shoulders and shook me. Shook me so hard! Then with a crazy, weird laugh, he said that he'd rather kill me and put me six feet under than divorce me.

I was shocked. I became numb. And at that moment, I knew I was dealing with a dangerous man. I didn't say a word.

He said, *"Don't ever, ever ask me that again if you want to stay alive."*

I became numb on that day and I stayed numb for the rest of the time we were together. I was numb. The next day, I had our son.

As mothers, especially in certain African cultures, there is a strong belief that a woman should stay with her husband no matter what because it's better for children to have their father in their life than not to have a father in their life. This belief has nothing to do with the Muslim religion. It's people misrepresenting the Muslim religion to promote a cultural standard.

At the time, I thought since I grew up without a father, I didn't want my children to grow up without their father. I had our son and I made a decision that I was going to take care of our son and I was going to take care of myself. I grew up without a father and I thought that if I stayed away from my husband and his issues and focused on myself, I could raise our son.

Less than a year later I gave birth to our daughter. We were still homeless. I had to find stable housing on my own. I saved money and rented an apartment for us. I told my husband I was sick and tired of the way he treated me, that I was working and paying all the bills, plus buying groceries, cooking and cleaning, taking the kids to daycare, doctor's appointments, everything. I felt like the husband, wife, mother, *and* provider. I was exhausted, depressed and angry. Even though I knew he was dangerous, I also knew I couldn't keep living like this. I told my husband that if he didn't change and start helping me, that we needed to get divorced.

Every time we had this argument, he would get objects like scissors or knives and use them to threaten me. He would take a big knife out of the drawer while we were talking and start to sharpen it. One night, he cut off a piece of my hair while I slept and left it on top of the dresser with the scissors next to it. Another night he put metal objects under my pillow to scare me. He terrorized me to my core because he took my power from me by his words and actions.

My husband was a very dangerous man because he could be extremely charming and kind and was well-liked by everyone in the community. But at home he was a manipulative, abusive pathological liar. He molested two of my sisters while I was married to him. When I found out about the molestation, I couldn't be married to him anymore.

It was a terrifying situation and I felt voiceless. I had no male protection—siblings or uncles—that he was afraid of. The only males in my life were my brothers and my stepfather who always sided with him, even though my husband had molested my sisters! I could not understand how a father could take the side of a man who molested his own daughters.

I felt afraid and despondent. How could this happen to me? How did I wind up in this awful place? I was shocked and confused. I felt so many different emotions that I didn't know who I was. By the time I summoned up the courage to kick my husband out, my stepfather shocked me again by taking *my* side. At least, he told me he would help me.

He told me I should kick my husband out and said that he would change the locks. It gave me so much courage when I thought my stepfather was on my side. He told me he would come to my workplace to get money to buy a new lock. Then, he would change the lock and bring me the keys, so when my husband got home, his key wouldn't work and he wouldn't be able to get in.

I was excited. I was hopeful. I was still terrified but less so because I thought my stepfather was on my side. My stepfather changed the locks and brought me the new keys. Still, I was afraid I wouldn't be safe. I knew what kind of man my husband was. I was certain that he would break the window and come into the house that way. I packed some clothes for my children and myself so we could stay away from the house for a few days.

When my husband came home late that night and his key didn't work, he looked for me in the only place he thought I would be—staying with my auntie who babysat our kids. I was young, so I wasn't smart enough to *not* be there. I thought I would sleep at my auntie's house and go to work in the morning. My car was parked outside.

It was around one o'clock in the morning when my husband started banging on the door. My auntie told him to leave or she would call the police.

He yelled, *"I know she's here; her car's here! I know you have her and the kids, open the door!"*

My brave auntie told him *"No, you need to find a place to sleep overnight and take care of yourself, go to your friends or go to a hotel or do something else."* Instead of going somewhere, he went back to our house, broke the window, got into the house, and went to sleep.

The next morning he called my stepfather. He told him that I had locked him out of the house, he had broken a window to get in, and didn't know what to do now. My stepfather acted like he didn't know anything about it. He said, let me call her and find out what's going on.

My stepfather called me laughing—literally laughing—telling me the stupid guy went to the house and broke the window and now he's looking for you and he wants to know why you did that. I was shocked and speechless. I told my stepfather that he knew the reason we locked him out. I asked him to tell my husband not to come back to the house. And that if my husband didn't want me to call the police, he needed to fix the window and leave the house.

My stepfather called him back and told him, *"She's threatening you, she's going to call the police if you don't fix the window. So before she does that, I'm going to help you fix the window and I want you to bring your stuff and come stay with me."*

My stepfather invited my husband to stay with them knowing that he had molested two of his daughters! After offering to help me, my step father took him in! My only male protector and supporter, *took him in*. I was terrified and so shaken—there was no safety anywhere, it seemed. I thought, *"What world am I living in?"* I was not safe. None of us were safe.

In other places in the world, families won't allow a man to harm a woman. Where I am from in Somalia, men don't touch women. Instead, they protect them. A husband has no right to physically harm his wife. If he does, he will pay. Her family will beat him and make him regret abusing a woman.

Where I am from in Somalia, domestic violence usually happens when the woman or girl doesn't have protection, when the woman doesn't have male family members in her life. Back home, if a woman doesn't have a family, it's really hard on her and her children. Women cannot have male friends in our culture, so that's not a possibility for male protection either.

In other regions of Somalia, domestic violence is accepted. People say things like, *"He's disciplining his wife."* It's not condemned. This system is unjust and very dangerous for women.

My husband stayed at my mother and stepfather's place for a few days, calling me constantly. He told people in our community that I locked him out and he was staying with my mother and stepfather. He told me he wanted his family back.

I told him *"No, I can't."* I was scared for myself, terrified. He had molested my sisters and threatened my life. A few days after I locked him out, he called one of my friends and told her that I was waiting for him. Since he didn't have a car, he asked if her husband could pick him up.

My friend's husband picked him up and brought him to my house.When I heard the knock, I peeked out the window. I relaxed when I saw my best friend's husband's car, never imagining that it was my ex-husband. I opened the door, excited and hoping it was my friend. That's when my husband grabbed my hair and neck and beat me up. *He beat from the neck up like a snake.*

I was fighting so hard. And I was screaming. My best friend's husband was sitting in his car on the phone with his wife and she heard me screaming. She told her husband, *"Fatoun is screaming!"* So he started running upstairs to the house.

My husband beat me so badly, I lost consciousness. I lost a lot of blood. I was bleeding and had passed out. My friend's husband told him, *"Run, run, run!"* He left the house. He ran. *He left me for dead.*

While her husband was trying to make sure I was alive, my best friend came over and took me to the emergency room. But first she covered me up with a hijab, from my forehead to my neck because I had scratches all over my neck, multiple bumps on my head, and she did not want the nurse to see those. She told me not to report my husband, not to say anything.

She said, *"We have to protect our children, we have to protect him, he's the father of your children, he's your husband. It would be a shame; we don't want him to be arrested and have a criminal record. Please, we can solve this as a community; don't report it."*

I was sort of aware of what was happening, but I was lost and confused, bleeding everywhere. So I said, *"Okay."*

She took me to the emergency department. The nurse asked me what happened. My friend had prepped me; told me to say that I fell in the bathroom. So that's what I told the nurse.

The nurse said, *"Hmm, you fell in the bathroom and this is what happened to you?"*

I said, *"Yes, I fell and hurt my head in the shower."*

The nurse said, *"Women like you who cover for your abuser end up six feet under and we bury them."*

I was shocked by her reply. Because that was what my husband was planning. He had used the same words: he was going to put me six feet under. I was out of it for three weeks. When I woke up, I realized what had happened.

There was a huge, huge wake-up call for me. I thought, *"Oh my God, what if I had just died when he beat me up and left me for dead? If he had killed me, what would happen to my son? What would happen to my daughter? What kind of life would they have without me, knowing that their mom was dead by their father's hand?"*

He'd either be in prison or nowhere to be found. My mom would cry; she would say *"I lost my daughter!"* My siblings would cry; they would be upset. The community would get together, they would bury me, they would grieve for a minute, but they would forget about me in a few weeks, in a few months, in a few years.

But the people that would never be the same, whose lives would be forever changed, who would not have a mother in their lives, would be my two children. That's when I decided I needed to live for them, raise them, and protect them. I needed to be here for them. I could not afford for him to ever touch me again.

And that's when I decided I was going to save my life; I was going to get a divorce from him, no matter what. At the same time, it was hard. It was really hard. Living with my husband was like living with the devil. He manipulated me and made me feel like I was the crazy one. I doubted my reality when he was near. All of my energy went to trying to predict how he was going to behave. I became numb to anything that he did to me, because I was too exhausted and scared to confront it. Also, I was terrified of what would happen to my kids if I tried to leave.

Finally, the whole situation got too violent to stay any longer. When my husband beat me that last time, I knew I would die if I stayed. I started planning: how do I escape? Thank Allah that in this country, in America and the Western world, there are so many options.

You can call a local women's shelter or a domestic abuse hotline, there are free services, there are county agencies that are willing to help single mothers. For me, my personal story, I escaped by not trusting anyone because the people I trusted had betrayed my trust.

So I kept quiet and made a plan.

The first thing I did was to think critically about the situation and how I was going to move. Then I called my work and asked my boss to write me a letter of recommendation. She wrote me a beautiful letter. Next, I asked my landlord for a letter as well. I was always on time with rent and had never missed a payment. So they gave me a letter of recommendation also.

I went to my tax preparer and got copies of my tax returns from the previous two years. And then I went to the library and I updated my resume. (Except for the address because I didn't have a new address yet.)

The only resource I had was my gold. I bonded my gold, which means I got a high-interest loan using my gold as collateral. If I paid off the loan on time, I would get my gold back. Thank God, I had enough gold that I got a loan of

$10,000 in cash. I took my cash hoping that I would get my gold back sometime in the future. Hoping I could get a job and get my gold back. It didn't happen that way. I lost my gold, but my $10,000 saved me and my children. They were two and three years old.

I gave the required thirty days notice to my landlord while I was putting everything together. I rented a storage unit. When I knew there were no people around and no one could see me, I hired two guys to help me pack most of my stuff and store it. I went to U-Haul, rented a truck, and got boxes. I put everything in the boxes, marked them, and I put them in storage. I tried to get a plane ticket, but my doctor said that, due to my injury, I couldn't fly.

Instead, I got a train ticket. I rented a room on the train and went to Minneapolis with my two children and two suitcases. Before I left California, I rented a hotel room in Minneapolis next to the Amtrak station. I had only one friend in Minnesota.

I called my friend and I said, "I'm on my way. Don't tell anybody". That's how I escaped. I trusted my friend in Minnesota. She was on my side. She didn't like men who abuse, and she knew my situation. I had already taken a trip to Minnesota for two weeks to look around. That was part of my planning. I had looked around the city, and checked out the people and the community.

I had been trying to decide between moving to Seattle, Washington, where I would be close to my auntie, or Minneapolis, where I only had one friend. I wanted to be close to my community, but at the same time, I didn't want anybody to know my plan.

The minute I stepped off the train with my children, we took a taxi and went to our hotel. The next morning, I reserved a rental car, got a taxi to the local Walmart to buy car seats for my children, and found the local library.

At the library, I did a Google search to find out where the Somali community and Somali malls were. My children and I went to the Somali mall. As we walked around, I saw a woman in her 60s, and asked her if she knew of any apartments for rent in the area.

At first, she said *"No."* Then she said, *"Wait, wait, wait! There's an apartment in Midtown Exchange on Lake Street and Chicago."* The building was new at that time.

So I said, *"I don't know where that is. Is there a way that you or someone can go with me to show me the place?"* And she found a young person to go with me, but when we got there, it was closed. I got the apartment contact information and went back to my hotel. The next morning, I called the apartment manager, and they told me to come back. I told them my situation, how I was new to the state, that I was running away from domestic violence, and had a letter of recommendation from my previous landlord.

I told them I also had my tax returns, a deposit, and the first month's rent, and that I was applying for county assistance as soon as I had an address.

A week later, they called me and said, *"You've got an apartment."* Once I got into my apartment, I applied for financial assistance, child care assistance, food stamps, medical assistance, and cash assistance for gas and utilities until I got a job . From there on, I kept on improving my life, one step at a time.

Here's what to do first to find safety

Sometimes you're in such a low place, it's hard to even know where to start or how to identify and locate resources, because often your abuser will make sure that you feel isolated, depressed, and like you can't live or even survive without them. Like they're all you have.

That's what my *third* husband did. (It took me a long time to change my pattern of attracting and committing to men who hurt me.) He said things like, *"Who's going to want you? I married you with two kids. Who's going to marry you with four kids? You better keep me. You have no other options."*

He belittled me, made me feel so small. He made me feel like a second-class citizen. He told me that no other Somali would want me or need me or look at me because I'm from a minority tribe.

He said, *"You're uneducated. You claim to be Somali, but you cannot read or write Somali. You claim to be Muslim, but you are using credit cards which have interest, shaming you. It's haram. It's against our religion. What kind of Muslim are you? You're going to hell."*

He used every insult that he thought would keep me under his thumb.. He told me *"Prophet Muhammad said you marry a wife based on four things—her wealth, her beauty, her youth, or her tribe—and you don't have any of them."*

In addition to the abuser's tactics, the community pressure to stay with an abusive husband is extreme. *"For the sake of the children,"* that's what people say. *"For the sake of the children, you can't afford to be a single mother."* But the truth is, it's not healthy or good or even safe for children to grow up in an abusive household. Because when you're not safe or healthy, your children are not safe or healthy either. Even if you're not raising children, it's far better to be healthy, happy, and alone than be depressed, abused, and at risk.

If you know you won't get support in leaving an abusive situation from your family and immediate circle, it might be helpful to talk with someone outside of your immediate community. Find a friend or trusted co-worker that none of your family or friends know, and ask them to help you look for resources. For safety's sake, choose someone who is well-known in the community, a professional person who is well-established.

If you're not safe at home, start by quietly, privately identifying the resources that are available so you can make a plan. One really good way to get started is to make an appointment to see your doctor (or any doctor, if you don't yet have one) and go to the appointment by yourself.

In the bathroom of many doctor's offices, they have posters asking if you're being abused, if you feel safe at home. Even if they don't have a poster, you can simply tell your doctor or nurse that you're trying to leave an abusive relationship and they will help connect you to community resources.

Because of patient confidentiality rules, the doctor is not going to tell your family your problems. Tell the medical staff you're in an abusive relationship, that you don't feel safe, you're depressed, you're sad, and you are seeking help.

They will offer confidential resources and guidance, like county programs, women's shelters, and domestic abuse hotlines. Even if you have to leave the city or state, do so for the sake of your safety and health.

It's okay to seek help

If you're dealing with debilitating depression, trauma, or grief, I can assure you from personal experience that counseling and therapy can help. In the Somali community, there is a widespread stigma against seeking counseling as many consider it a sign of moral weakness or a lack of faith. You might hear that getting counseling is proof that you're not a good Muslim.

But mental health and being abused have *nothing* to do with faith or religion or God! As I wrote about at length in Chapter 6, the stigma against counseling is a lack of understanding at best and a deliberate manipulation at worst. Finding a supportive mental health provider can be key in helping women find the strength to get out of a toxic relationship. What I learned in therapy changed my life; it can change yours as well.

If you're in an abusive relationship, know that you *can* have a better life. You can rediscover and reclaim your strength and inner power. You can set goals, follow your dreams, go to school, have a career. You can create a safe and healthy home for your children. You can be successful and happy.

Know that your past does not define who you are and it does not limit your potential of who you can become.

Divorce within the Muslim religion

In our religion, a woman cannot divorce a man. She can *request* a divorce. Like me, for example. I chose to get divorced. I made sure I got divorced.

I refused to tolerate any sort of abuse: mental, physical, emotional, financial, verbal, psychological, sexual, or spiritual. I also refused to settle for less and have abusive, manipulative, narcissistic control freaks in my life. Life is too short to live a toxic and unhealthy life! I choose to live in a healthy environment, create healthy relationships, have peace of mind, and be happy.

I refused to stay married to each of my husbands for different reasons: one was not being responsible. He was using drugs, drinking alcohol, and did not provide for me. We couldn't have healthy children together due to having the same genes. The other two husbands were not being responsible providers either and were also abusing me physically, mentally, and emotionally.

In the Muslim religion, if a husband is not providing for his wife, if he's not taking care of her, or if he is in any way emotionally or physically abusing her, and the Imam believes her life is threatened, he will grant a divorce to the woman with witnesses.

In my case, even though my first husband wasn't responsible and didn't provide for our family, he preferred to see me happy rather than miserable. It took him a year and a half to be okay with it, but he did finally agree to a divorce.

In my second marriage, they made him divorce me. In front of him, and with my brother and three other men as witnesses, the two imams granted my divorce. But the imams did not grant my divorce right away. They told me I had to give him a chance, regardless of the beating, regardless of the abuse, regardless of everything.

When we first went to them for the divorce, they told us we had to start with mediation.
Even though they knew what he did was wrong, he apologized, and there were witnesses, they said that he should be grateful that I didn't report him to the police.

They told me I was going to have to give my husband a chance and see if he improved. He promised that he was going to change. I knew that he would not change, but I agreed to give him thirty days to change his behavior if he wanted to keep his family.

They also set a list of standards he needed to meet, like:

- Take the responsibility of paying the household bills, including rent and utilities.
- Provide for the family and help with the children.
- Apologize to my parents for what he did.
- Pay me $5,000 restitution for the pain and suffering he caused by beating me up, for the blood, and for me not reporting him to the police.

He promised he would do all that, pay the rent and utility bills, apologize to my family, help with the children, and pay me $5,000 restitution. All within thirty days. He agreed to that.
I agreed as well, even though I knew he wasn't capable of doing that.

I convinced them to promise, to guarantee that the divorce would automatically be granted on the thirtieth day if he didn't follow through and change his behavior. I got them to swear on God's name, with each other as witnesses.

My husband never changed, not even a minute, not even one thing. He didn't apologize, he didn't work, he didn't provide, he didn't help me with the children, he didn't give me any money. On the twenty-ninth day, we had just dropped my cousin off at the airport when my husband spat in my face while driving down the highway and said, *"I cannot do this anymore."*

I know he was thinking about the next day. He said, *"I'm done. I am done. Let's go to the mosque."* We went to the mosque that day but the imams were not there because our appointment was the next day. When we got home, my husband took all his stuff and left the house. The next day he showed up at the mosque and they granted me my divorce.

I didn't want just a verbal divorce. I wanted it to be in writing. I wanted it signed by the imams, with the mosque's official stamp. Because he was physically abusing me, and because he left me for dead, the imams were afraid for my safety. And he wasn't providing for our family at all. So, they granted my divorce in front of him while he sat there powerless.

Because he had respect for the religious leaders, and he understood that they knew he hadn't done what he was supposed to do. I had male protection in this instance. He couldn't fight them. So the religious leaders have to look at each individual situation.

But in the Muslim religion, men can divorce women simply if they choose to. If a man is not happy with his wife for any reason, he can just tell her in writing or even verbally in front of a couple of witnesses that he is divorcing her. Men don't have to go through court; they don't have to do much. But for the women, it's a process.

If you're in an abusive relationship, know that you have choices, my Dear Sister. Taking even one step to get to safety can set a new life in motion for you. Beware your own tendency to want to stick with what's comfortable and familiar over what is safest and best for you. Leaving can be so hard even when it's what you want and need, because we've been conditioned to do what our culture says is right, not what we know is right for us and our children.

Your brain may also be your enemy for a time as you are planning to leave. Our brains crave what they know. Sometimes it can feel easier and safer to stay in a familiar situation, even if you know it's unsafe for you and your kids. Getting help and support can help you leave for good—where real safety can take hold and where you can work on setting goals for yourself for the life you truly want.

How to make a plan to leave

- First, tell the truth about the abuse to yourself. Stop minimizing what is happening or making excuses for your husband. Break through your own denial. This behavior will not change. The abuse will continue and you or your children may not survive it unless you can get out.
- Find someone you trust outside of your family, like a medical doctor, who can help you find the resources you need to leave, like money, a place to live, and safe care for your children.
- Keep your plan to leave quiet, at least until you actually get out. After making a plan for how to survive after you leave, find the right moment, and do it.
- Cut ties to the people who know and support your abuser (like changing your phone number or email address and social media accounts.)

Questions to help you get out of a toxic relationship:

- Are you being physically, verbally, or emotionally abused by anyone in your life?

____

____

____

____

____

____

____

____

____

____

____

____

- Do you have a family doctor or medical clinic? If not, now is the time to locate one and schedule an appointment. Doctors and medical staff are often the first professionals to help women who are being abused find safety.

- Do you have the contact information (phone number, street address) of your local social services agency? This is usually your county government.

~~~
~~~

My Invaluable Sisters, you are strong, creative, and loving. Your life is important. YOU are important! Whether or not you're raising children, it's better to be healthy, happy, alone, and safe than with someone who abuses, threatens, or belittles you and makes you fearful, depressed, sad, anxious, and exhausted. You can do this. And you don't have to do it alone.

PART III.
CULTIVATE HEALTHY, SUPPORTIVE RELATIONSHIPS WITH OTHERS

Chapter 14

Cultivate Healthy, Supportive Relationships with Your Friends, Neighbors, and Community

Extended family to me are the people that feed my soul and my heart and the people that help me throughout my life that I consider my family of choice. It's so important to spend time with the people you love.

The other morning, I had breakfast with my friend Marilyn. She made me a delicious meal. We talked, we laughed, we cried, we had so much fun. She's not my mother. She's in her 70s. She's a white woman, cooking breakfast for me. It's just amazing.

Throughout the book, I am calling you, Sister, and I want you to believe that you are my Dear Sister for many reasons. I want you to know the true meaning of a sister and sisterhood. A sister is a gift from Allah, (God), she is a true best friend to have.

She cries with you, she is a secret keeper, she listens to your crazy stories, she encourages you, she uplifts your spirit, she soothes your soul, she is a supporter, she is a protector, she is there for you when you need her. She guides you and inspires you. She laughs and fights with you and tells you the truth. And you do all those same things for her. When I think of a sister, I get warmth in my heart–a comforting feeling of care, love and nourishment.

It's crucial to learn how to make and keep good friends—women who feel like sisters to you. This is not something we are taught in our culture. We compete with other women, and we are not allowed to be friends with men, which only results in us being lonely, isolated, sad, overwhelmed, sometimes, with our children and being a parent, and even trapped in dangerous situations.

When we have good friends we can trust, it's possible to envision and live a wonderful life of satisfaction. Friends mean safety and enrichment. They mean you can feel connected and supported. They mean you can feel nourished and uplifted in your life. But if you don't know the first thing about making a friend, it can be really hard to get started. In this chapter, we'll cover how to take the first steps in creating a network of friends you can come to love and trust like family.

Supporting each other in our culture is one more way we can make life better, easier, healthier and valuable for ALL of our Dear Sisters. When one of us starts to heal, nurture, nourish, and better herself, let that be an inspiration to all of us to keep making change—in ourselves, our families, and our communities!

What kind of friends to have in your life

I was talking to my therapist the other day, and I was telling her that when I was in San Diego, I had three wonderful women who stepped up to be like mothers to me. When I moved to Minneapolis, I wanted to find a good friend here as quickly as possible. I wanted to meet someone a little older than me, because I felt like people my age didn't have the experience or wisdom I needed in my life.

When I reached out to Somali women in Minnesota who were older and around my mom's age, what I encountered was devastating. One of the older Somali women I met tried to prostitute me. She introduced me to an older Somali man who had a lot of money. He came to the United States in the 1970s and established himself very well. The woman I met wanted to get some money from him, and she thought I was going to be the way that happened.

Meanwhile, I was new to the city, started my business and a nonprofit company, enrolled in school, and was raising my two young kids. This man saw potential in me that the older woman did not, and confided in me what her real intentions were for the introduction. I quickly decided I did not need women in my life like her! I was lucky to have gotten out of the situation without being violated.

This man wound up being kind to me and warning me about the kind of people to watch out for in this new city. He came to my office and admired my work and saw me struggling and he helped me out.

He said, *"Try to stay away from those people. I'm going to tell you who she is and how she wanted me to use you."* It was just devastating.

There are some such predatory women in our community, and not only for prostitution. Vulnerable Somali women (who might be homeless, single mothers, or struggling to feed themselves and their family) can fall into the trap of trading slave labor (like babysitting, house cleaning, or cooking) for the scraps and crumbs they need to survive. Predatory women may also try to get their vulnerable targets to use drugs and become addicted, further cementing the abusive relationship. These people are not your friends. Be watchful.

This horrible experience happened to me while I was trying to find my way in a new city with my young family, even to the point of offering to trade food stamps I got to feed my family for drugs. I had fallen in with a group of other Somali immigrants who were trying to get money for drugs. It was so hard to know who I could trust!

I had to cut these terrible people out of my life, even though I had no one else at the time. Loneliness can make you accept things in your life that are only bad for you in the long run. When we are not lonely, it's so much easier to make good, healthy decisions for yourself and your children. It didn't matter how lonely I felt, how sad I felt, how depressed I felt. I had to get out of that circle of people. I had to go out of my community to feel safe.

A lot of young Somali women don't have that opportunity or wouldn't even know to look for it. It's easy to believe that because someone looks and speaks like you, they must be safe to have in your life. It's crucial to get to know everyone you want to allow in your life individually. Let them prove themselves to you first, no matter what they look like, what language they speak, or where they're from.

Here's how to know if someone could be a good friend to you:

1. They don't hurt you or want to hurt you, physically, emotionally, financially, or sexually.
2. They don't take advantage of your kindness or generosity, or your vulnerable situation.
3. They support you in times of trouble, but also let you find your way through with your own strength and knowledge.
4. They are honest with you and concerned for you.
5. If you need something and they can provide it with a happy heart and open hands, they do.
6. They want to know about you and how you're feeling.
7. They let you talk to them when you're struggling, and they listen deeply.
8. They care about your family.
9. They give you strength and warmth, not judgment and cruelty.

Women and competition

Many women, whether Somali or not, feel the need to compete with each other. We "swim" in these feelings and sometimes obsessions because of our learned value in our culture. Our culture says we are only valuable if we can have babies (and especially boys), we are young, pretty, have lighter skin, are well-dressed, and draped in expensive jewelry, or have a "better" husband. The practice of plural marriage (multiple wives) is what creates this competition. Women are always looking over their shoulders, afraid of being replaced.

There is also the view that men are in short supply. This story is false. There are plenty of men out there—good ones who value the women they love. When you do not need a man to survive and you know your own value within, there is no need to compete.

Where are *we* in this scenario? The only people who benefit from Somali women competing with each other are the men who have devalued us for generations. As long as we compete among ourselves, nothing will change. Our cultural value will not change.

When we befriend one another in healthy and trusting relationships, we get *value from that.* And it's a value *we created for ourselves.* We do not need men to validate us when we support each other. And when we don't need a man to think we are attractive and worthy, we empower ourselves to rise up, stop settling for abusive relationships, and improve our lives and the lives of our children.

I learned that since moving to Minnesota in 2006, I've accomplished something every year. Whether it was getting my college degree, running my own business, or changing the way I parent my kids, those accomplishments started giving me *value* I could feel from within. I have never competed with my Dear Sisters–I could start lifting them up, too!

I made a decision. After seeing so many of my cousins competing with each other, I made a conscious choice that I will never compete with a woman or another human being. I am my own competition. I have only myself to compete against, which simply means I have to be a better person today than I was yesterday. It doesn't matter if someone looks better than I do, or has more money or children or education, or if they're married. It doesn't matter how they got there. Jealousy and competition with others will only kill your goals and your momentum.

Competition shows up in these ways with the people I know:

- Comparing who is wearing the most expensive dress.
- Announcing how much you spent on your makeup or henna.
- Who has a bigger house, newer furniture, nicer car, or more gold.
- Sharing the price of your latest dirca.
- Feeling pressured to "keep up" with your community by spending money you do not have on expensive jewelry, dresses, makeup, or other possessions, especially for community weddings.

My Dear Sister, it is wonderful to be able to spend money on yourself, to feel beautiful, to feel worthy. Women should dress in ways that help them feel confident and gorgeous as often as they can. But if you're spending money on a dress you'll only wear once, or announcing how much your makeup cost, who are you trying to impress? The only person you need to please with the way you look is *you,* no matter how much you spend.

I remember one particular time, a neighbor of mine bragged that she spent over $2000 on herself. One evening, I took us to a photoshoot just for fun–I spent about $125 on me. My neighbor kept saying *"Oh my God, you look good. You look better than me!"*

She told me her dress was $1500. Her hair cost this, her makeup cost that, not to mention the gold jewelry she wore.

I thought, *"Oh my God!"* I got a simple but lovely dirca that looked good on me–it was a beautiful color. It was about $120. I got henna for my fingertips and my daughter did my makeup for me in a simple way that made me look and feel beautiful. Plus, I'll feel proud to wear my beautiful dress again, because it looks good on me and I enjoy how I feel when I wear it. I don't care whether others have seen it. Simple and natural is the way I like to go—wearing little makeup because it's better for my skin.

We don't have to wear ourselves out or spend a lot of money to show our value. When our value comes from inside, it's a lot more comfortable to live without competing with our Dear Sisters.

And I want every woman to sit with herself. I want her to ask herself *"Why am I competing? Why do I feel like I have to compete?"* When you're acting this way, why are you doing it? When you're talking this way, why are you doing it? When you are backstabbing and talking about other women, how do you truly feel inside?

If you speak badly of someone else so that you can feel better or more valuable, why do you feel like you have to do that? How do you think your actions and words affect others? Will you really gain anything by competing?

Tips for stopping competition:

- Write down your answers to the questions above—how are you benefitting from competing?
- When you attend your next wedding and want to buy a dress, carefully look at your household budget and think ahead. How much money can you afford to spend on a new dress without taking away from your other needs?
- Go shopping on your own—not with other women!
- Buy in bulk—with new clothing, try to purchase a few Dirca at once that have designs and colors you will enjoy and feel good wearing often.
- Pool your money with other Sisters—purchase clothing and jewelry in bulk, and then borrow and trade with your Sisters so that you all have "new" clothes when you get bored with your existing dresses, even though they are still beautiful.

Real life tips for finding your Sisters:

Even if you agree that having a supportive community of Sisters would feel wonderful to you, it can feel impossible to find them. Here are a few ways you can begin:

- Look for a Women's Interfaith Group in your community (try searching "Women's Interfaith Group near me" online as a start.)
- Join networking groups for business owners and other professionals.
- Ask around your Mosque for groups of women who gather regularly to support and encourage one another.
- Check the local library for book clubs or discussion groups.
- Go to www.meetup.com and look for groups on hobbies you're interested in, business meetups, and groups specific to the Muslim faith.

Growth is not easy. You'll have to be brave and get out there. Not every group you try will be the right fit. You'll feel awkward, you'll feel nervous at first. It's natural to feel afraid around people who don't look like you, speak your native language, or have your same religion. Give yourself time and a lot of trial and error. Be just vulnerable enough to share a story or two about yourself. That is where connection and trust happen.

It's true that you have to be careful. Just like in the story I told earlier, toxic and unsafe people are out there. Trust your gut. If something doesn't feel right, run away from it. But then keep trying and keep connecting. The Sisters you fit with will find you. You have to keep looking for them. Life is all about growth and learning. When you see the journey of sisterhood as a learning process, it can become less scary and more exciting!

Questions to help you find your Sisters:

1. **What does it mean to you to have a trustworthy sister in your life?**

   ____

   ____

   ____

   ____

   ____

   ____

2. **Are you open to having a sister that does not look like you or does not have the same religion as you?**

   ____

   ____

   ____

   ____

   ____

3. **Can you be a sister to a woman that needs a sister in her life?**

____

____

____

____

____

~~~

My Faithful Sisters, I need to share how important it is to have a Sister in your life, whether she is your biological sister or not. It is crucial to have a nurturing, supportive Sister who is always there for you. If you don't have a supportive sister in your family or community, you can definitely create your own sisterhood club. Believe me, I have done it, I have the most beautiful, supportive and loving sisters in my life. They are always there for me, in the good times, the bad times, and the ugly times. There are so many wonderful sisters out there who are waiting to hold hands and walk with you, to love you, nurture you and support you. Step out of your comfort zone and find your loving community. It's waiting for you, I promise.
~~~

Chapter 15

How to Address Discrimination and Tribalism

I am from what is considered a minority tribe in Somalia, the Yibir clan. There's still a lot of discrimination against certain tribes within Somalia and also within the U.S. Somali communities. The tribal discrimination is devastating and sometimes deadly. It has destroyed many lives.

I grew up questioning why this is. We have been discriminated against for as long as I can remember. Some people are afraid of us. Some consider the Yibirs to be Jewish, not Somalis, even if we follow the Muslim faith.

For example, back when I was growing up in Somalia in the late 1980s, people from the majority tribes would not marry people from Somali minority tribes.That's still true today. If a man and woman from different tribes fell in love and decided to get married, they were literally putting their lives at risk, along with being shunned, disowned, and tormented by the majority tribe family. The majority tribe's father, brothers, uncles, even mother and aunties would do whatever they could to make the young couple miserable, especially the one from the minority tribe. I have heard about young women who are so desperate to be with the man they love that they will do anything to be with him, even risking being killed by their family. Or taking their own life.

My cousin, Rasheed Farrah, Ed. D., summarizes the problem of tribalism and possible solutions in his dissertation, A STUDY OF THE INDIGENOUS MINORITIES OF SOMALILAND: FOCUS ON BARRIERS TO EDUCATION:

PROBLEM: In Somalia, the members of Yibir, Gaboye, and Tumal ethnic minorities are physically, culturally, religiously, and linguistically indistinguishable from other dominant groups. However, for two hundred years they have endured oppression, discrimination, and exclusion from all aspects of the Somali social, political, economic, and educational activities.

Yibir, Gaboye, and Tumal children continue to face educational barriers including bullying, discrimination, and alienation. This study investigated key factors that contributed to the educational barriers of 24 young adults from the indigenous minorities of Somaliland.

RESULTS: The purpose of this study was to examine the Yibir, Gaboye and Tumal young adult's perceived barriers to education in Somaliland, and to generate a theory about their views. The common themes of educational barriers were bullying, verbal, and physical abuse, ethnic harassment, discrimination, fear of negative treatment by other students, and overall alienation.

Additional barriers identified included distance to schools, lack of parent encouragement, lack of supportive programs for minorities, and lack of retention programs. Regarding the impact of the lack of education on their current lifestyle, the participants cited low social-economic living conditions, inadequate job skills, and a high rate of unemployment.

The emerged theory proposes that in the absence of supportive educational programs such as human rights education, and /or legal laws that are designed to combat discrimination against ethnic minorities in Somaliland, barriers to their education will remain in place.

I believe Somalia will never be stable or have peace as long as the discrimination against minorities continues. Depending even on which region of the cities people are from, they are treated differently. I remember in 2005 a minority man was shot and killed right outside his own store just because a military man felt like it. The store owner was smoking outside his store and the military man shot him.

If you're a member of a minority tribe, you can be killed as if you're not even a human being. This is true especially if you're a man, and even more so if you're a young man, *because men are more involved in the community in general and are more likely to interact with people from majority tribes than women or children are.* When someone from a minority tribe gets killed by someone from a majority tribe, there is no justice. There's no arrest, no prosecution, no consequences for majority tribes because they have all the political power and make all the laws.

Most Somali minorities didn't or don't have the opportunity to get a higher education, or the opportunity to get into government jobs. For those that did somehow beat the system, their lives were often made unbearable. They were not able to make any significant change for themselves and other minorities.

It's not only those from minority tribes who suffer in Somalia. Those who are the most vulnerable and have no way of defending themselves also suffer greatly from injustice and discrimination: orphans, the elderly, people with disabilities, people with mental illnesses… I have seen it and I have witnessed it. There is a lack of compassion, a lack of kindness. Even animals are treated poorly.

I believe that for lasting change to happen in Somalia, leaders in the community—religious leaders, those in government, educators, doctors, lawyers — need to put their egos and tribalism aside and step up for the good of the country. They need to fight for justice and for the rights of all human beings.

Recently, I was working with the people who are helping me refine my brand, and they asked me about my short-term and long-term goals. One of my long-term goals is to be a catalyst for change in Somalia: to help change policies and change how the Somali government treats its citizens. It makes me so sad and angry and disappointed that people in positions of power are not fighting for the most vulnerable and the most oppressed.

I am starting an education foundation in Somalia to help women get an education and start their own small businesses. I will establish a program of micro-grants that can help women start businesses and earn money.

I want to change Somali culture into one in which children are raised in a loving environment. I want to be part of creating a culture in which women and young girls, the elderly, the disabled, and members of minority tribes are respected and safe.

I want to help build a culture in which strong men are productive in their society, in their community, in their family, and in themselves, and where men are partners in creating a safe environment for women, whether it's their wives, mothers, grandmothers, sisters, daughters, or cousins.

We need to go back to our religion and treat women the way we are supposed to be treated, with love and respect. I want men to step up— and I want women to step up. But the only real way women can do so is if women own their power. *When women make their own money, they no longer need to depend on a man for their survival.*

In the Muslim faith, women are allowed to make money, we're allowed to get an education, we're allowed to think for ourselves, but *we need to step up and own our power.*

Owning our power

When we own our power, we can educate ourselves, make decisions, change our environment, and change our world!

We need to get out of the little boxes in which we're isolating ourselves. We must change the thinking that we're not capable of doing anything for ourselves. We do not need approval from a man who is not treating us the way we're supposed to be treated as the queens that we are.

God created us to use our minds and listen to our spirits, to use our natural gifts in a healthy, loving way, and to build a strong foundation for our lives. Charity begins at home. If our mothers nurture our souls, our fathers provide for us and protect us, and we get the education we deserve, the world will change.

I see and I believe and I feel it in my bones that Somalia and our Somali communities in the U.S. have to change.

Stop the racism, stop the discrimination, stop the tribalism. We need to create a country that has no tribal system. Unfortunately, the underlying attitudes and practices of discrimination towards fellow Somalis didn't stop once people arrived in North America.

Many individuals from majority tribes who came to the U.S., Canada and other European Countries presented themselves as being from a minority tribe so they could get the stability, opportunities, and citizenship offered in North America and Europe. And now, they're competing with people from Somali minority tribes for resources here in the U.S..

So I ask myself, who's the minority here? Is it okay to be a minority if it means getting some resources? In Minnesota, everyone from Somalia is in a minority group. It's very interesting to me to see majority tribes having the experience of being the minority in a culture.

Minority tribes were given emigration precedence over majority tribes because they were suffering disproportionately, due to the entrenched systematic discrimination against them in Somalia. In Somalia, minorities did not start wars. Minorities did not kill people. Minorities did not have weapons. They did not have land to fight over. They were not in positions of power. But they were the people most impacted by the wars and crime and corruption.

I have so many scars from this discrimination because I couldn't understand it. As Somalis, we all look alike. We speak one language. We have one religion. We are like a family tree with many branches.

A non-native person couldn't tell who's who. Even native Somalis wouldn't know who's who unless people knew the tribe. It's a fictional construct. It's based on nothing except people maintaining and hoarding power. I grew up questioning what makes me different? What makes you better?

What I've learned is, it's about abusing power. The majority tribes only have more power because they're bigger. They're not scattered; they're all in one place, most of them. That's all. It has nothing to do with being better. I learned by studying the situation because I wanted to understand this toxic reality. Discrimination and racism can persist if only the most powerful few have all the information. A large part of the minority struggle is about lack of knowledge.

The other struggle for minority tribes is location. They are small and scattered. Minorities also don't own land. We don't have people in the government and higher positions. We don't have education. We had no path to financial security or impact on the government or influence in our regions.

I remember living as a minority in unwelcoming places. I couldn't get an education, and I noticed that even the (minority) children that *could* afford to go to school were discriminated against. They were called names. They were mocked. They were beaten. The majority tribe children and teachers were making those children miserable to the point that they quit going to school.

The only choice for survival for many minority people was to create jobs for themselves. The amazing thing that came out of that is that many of those minority people became business entrepreneurs!

My grandmother was one such minority. She was a powerful woman who was a midwife. She was a healer. She did cupping. She gave massages. She could help women who could not have babies—they sought her out. My grandma created an environment in which every person who was sick would come and seek her help. She developed her own way of making money and becoming valuable to the community, and made a good living doing so.

She was a business-minded woman, her skills were really in-demand, and people looked up to her. I believe I inherited that entrepreneurial spirit from my grandmother and my mom's side of the family.

My grandma was so powerful within her community that on the day she died, the whole city shut down and they lowered the flag in her honor. I was a nine-year-old girl wondering why the city shut down over my grandmother's passing. I didn't understand at that age it was because she was so powerful. She had businesses, she had stores, she had orchards, and she had people working for her despite the tribal issue.

My grandfather (her husband) was a mechanic. He had a shop; he would fix people's cars. My grandparents were powerful. But at the same time, all those people in their community who needed them would not marry my aunties or my uncles because of the tribe we were from. And everybody knew what tribe we were from because they used to call us by our tribe name of instead of our family last name.

There are more than fourteen minority tribes in Somalia and they are immensely resourceful and courageous and hardworking. They created jobs from nothing. Farmers. Shoemakers. Barbers, blacksmiths, butchers. Healers and midwives.

They are also artists, poets and singers. Some of the most famous Somali singers are Somali minorities because of the way they express their feelings through songs. You can feel the pain in their voices. You can feel the pain in their words.

Here in the U.S., I find it interesting that people from the Somali majority tribes are having the same experience as the minority tribes in Somalia. With very few exceptions, they're *not* holding government positions. They're *not* the judges and lawyers and professors.

Here, majority tribe members have had to become creators. They've had to start their own businesses, or to work for someone else. For some, this is positive and transformative. They understand, now that they've experienced it themselves, that discrimination is wrong. And they're gaining empathy, sympathy, and feeling regret and sadness about the minority discrimination that is rampant in Somalia.

Now these empathetic majority tribe members are asking, *"How can we change it?"* Some are now saying that, *"Many of us are from the same lineage, the same fathers, and some of them want to claim us back, saying we did you wrong. We apologize. Old men created these issues and separated us. We are family, we're related. We have the same fathers and forefathers, we're the same people."*

Some of us from minority tribes accept that. But many are rejecting the invitation, saying, *"You've discriminated against us for* **generations**. *Why do you want to claim us now?"*

To me, it doesn't matter. What's done is done, we can only look ahead. I always felt sorry for people who are ignorant. At the end of the day, we're human beings, that's how I look at everything. We're human beings, whether you're white, black, Asian, Indian, whatever, you're a human being.

We have cultures and we have languages and we have heritages—but if, like me, you never felt wanted in your birthplace, you don't want to be claimed. I never felt like I belonged to my country. I never felt welcome there. I never felt wanted. I never felt comfortable. I never felt like I belonged anywhere.

When I came to North America, I wanted to find a place where I belonged, because for so many years, I didn't feel like I belonged to my family. In Somalia, they told me, *"You're not even Somali, you're Jewish, you don't belong in this country."*

I didn't feel like I belonged to Somali culture. I wasn't a white or Christian or American, so I didn't feel like I belonged to American culture. I didn't know who I was or where I fit in. I felt like I was just floating above my body, asking myself, "*Where is my space*? *Where do I belong?"*

My family was discriminated against in Somalia by other Somalis. Then we came to Canada, the U.K. and the U.S. and were discriminated against by Somalis here because of our tribal affiliation and by others in the U.S. because of the color of our skin and our religion. Here in America, the discrimination is usually more indirect, done behind your back, not right to your face. No matter if we're from a majority tribe or a minority tribe, America and the Western world see us as Muslim. Black. African. Immigrants.

A good place to begin in addressing discrimination is to do some self-reflection, *examine our own behavior, and ask ourselves some hard questions.* (This is for everyone, not only in Minnesota, but anywhere in the world.)

"Have I discriminated against my sisters? (By competing with them, putting them down, saying bad things about them to others, or denying them help I could've easily given?) Am I discriminating against others who are different from me? Am I treating other women, especially fellow immigrant women, with respect?"

Because we want to create a healthy environment for every woman. We want to live in peace. We want to align our behavior with our religious principles and create a better, more just world.

I believe that we're all equal. We were all born and we will all die. We breathe and we sleep and we eat. We're all human, we are beautiful, and we are made by Allah. So no one is better than me. And I am not better than anyone else. God created us and we will one day return to our God. That is my belief.

I ask myself, *"Who am I? Who am I?"*

And the truth is, I'm a woman. I'm a human being. I'm a black woman, I'm a Muslim woman, I am a Somali woman. I am a daughter, I am a sister, I am a wife, I am a mother, I am a cousin, I am an auntie, and I am a grandmother. That's what I identify with—all of that! Not by my tribe. So as a Somali person, when they ask you what your tribe is, they're already labeling you in one way or another.

But they can't label me because I'm a human being! God brought me to this earth. I'm an individual, I'm a giver, I'm a provider, I'm a protector. I love people, I do charity work, and that's who I am. I was born in Somalia, but my soul belongs to God and my body belongs to God and I will die and be buried six feet under, so I don't need to be claimed by anyone. My tribe does not define me and it doesn't benefit me when I die.

It's so sad that people use tribalism to discriminate. To justify treating other people unfairly. I don't know exactly why people discriminate, but I believe it's mostly because of ignorance. Ignorance and ego and trying to hold onto power.

One of the biggest reasons that I started to help immigrants, especially Somali minority immigrants, was to let them know that they're in America now, they have a voice, they can get an education.

In Somalia there were so many things that we couldn't have. Education was one of them. We couldn't marry people from majority tribes. We held no positions in higher government. We couldn't get a lot of things because of tribalism. We lived in the lowest of the low environments. And we all struggled and worked really hard to provide for our families in doing labor jobs. Very few people from the minority tribes had the leverage to build a secure life.

I see a lot of minority tribes in the U. S. that don't claim their tribe. They think they can run away from it. They're not telling their children the reality, the truth of their heritage. My fear is that they're brainwashing their children not to tell the truth.

I always tell my children, this is who you are, and you're loving, you're kind, you're a human being, God created you and no one is better than you. You can have whatever you want that you put your mind to.

Ending discrimination starts every day with you

One thing I learned as a woman, an immigrant woman, and a woman in business, and working with people in general, is you can't worry about what other people think.

People will think whatever they think. They will say whatever they think is right. They will have their own opinions on everything that you can think of. That's okay. Others might be uneducated. Ignorant. Narrow-minded. Some people seem to lack human feelings. Though we may wonder where their kindness, love, humanity, compassion, and generosity went, we won't likely change their thinking. People only evolve when they are ready.

I don't worry about people. I focus on my life and what I want to accomplish. I want to feel good about what I do: helping people, empowering people, encouraging people, sharing what I know about housing or resources from my nonprofit. I do my best. Doing my best makes me feel good, and by the end of the evening, at night, I sleep well. I sleep like a baby. I sleep like a baby because I know that I did my best.

Every day, I try to be humble and love people. I know that you can't please everybody. One thing is for sure, 100%, that you cannot please everybody. Focus on your own life instead and be your own competition. Be better than you were yesterday. Look forward to the future and think positively. Love the world.

The fact that you're living and breathing and alive and healthy and you have a place to live and you have a brain to think and you can evaluate your life and purpose–that is what's most important.

Questions to help you effectively address discrimination and tribalism:

- What does tribalism mean to you? Has your perspective changed since coming to the U.S.? In what ways?

- If you have been discriminated against, what are some empowering actions you can take or empowering perspectives you can adopt?

- Have you witnessed tribalism within the U.S. Somali community? Have you ever discriminated against a sister who looks like you? If so, what actions can you take to right that wrong?

____

____

____

____

____

~~~

My beautiful, self-assured sisters, hold tight to your roots, your culture, and your religion because once you know who you are and where you came from, you know where you are going. Be humble, stay grounded, and be honest to yourself because your roots are the foundation of who you are.

A closing wish for you, My Dear Sister

If you can take even one helpful hint, support, nourishment, or bit of solidarity from my story, I have reached my goal, my Dear Sister. From one valuable woman to another, it's time to imagine the lives we want and make them happen.

The bottom line of my story is that you don't have to accept what is unacceptable in your life. You can reach for better. You can reach for more. You can reach for exactly what you want (as soon as you discover what that is.)

If your life is turned upside down right now with abuse, feeling overwhelmed, numbness, sadness, fear, or desperation and despair, know that I am with you. I have been there, and I got out. You can get out, too. The start of your liberation is as simple as a short prayer to the God of your understanding. When you ask for help out loud, and then begin to listen for the answer and watch for the assistance, you will be amazed before you've hardly begun.

You have to work with God. When you start with even one small empowering action, your intention and effort will snowball in exactly the right time and result for you. You've come to this book–to my story for a reason. If you've read this far, the time could be now for your transformation into an empowered, loving, strong, healthy, abundant Sister who enjoys a life she loves.
~~~

I wrote this book for you. For my daughters, my grandkids, my sisters, my aunties. I am one role model. I'm here today to change the world for our girls. With our example, our girls can stand up for their rights and learn to love and value themselves. As women, we have so much to give. We have the power to change the world, because we are the ones who bring human beings into the world. We have to teach our men from a young age how to be men–protectors, providers, and companions. To feel love and tenderness as much as dominance and anger. Our men have so many wounds, too. It is up to women to create the men we want.

Creating what we want means using our newly-discovered power in good ways. We need to be watchful that we don't use our power to destroy other lives or destroy our men. Instead, we can nurture, guide, and empower them too, so that we can have strong family foundations, healthy connections to our children and partners, and thriving communities. Having power does not mean power *over someone else,* like women have experienced from men for so many generations. It means having power *with other people–so that everyone is strong, cared for, and confident in their lives and relationships.*

Be sure to check out the resource section of this book just after this chapter. You'll be directed to more resources—exactly the ones that helped me learn to think differently about my life and my values and my goals. Having that support was what I needed at the right time so that I could start to change my experience. When you change your insides, your outside experiences also begin to shift—perhaps almost imperceptibly at first. With time and focus, your life will evolve in the way you want, for the highest good of you first, then your family, and then your community.

The resource section will also let you know how to contact me and how to explore more ways to work with me as a mentor and guide, if and when you're ready.

Until then, my Dear Sister, be well, be strong, and know that you are not forgotten…that you belong…that you have all the value of the sun, moon, and stars put together. Allah sees it, and so do I.

Peace & Love,
–Fatoun.

Acknowledgements

I would like to acknowledge and thank the following people for their encouragement, support, mentorship and leadership for this book and my personal growth, including my family, my friends, and my community.

First, I am grateful to Allah almighty for giving me the strength, guidance and the wisdom to write this book and everything I have. My four beautiful, kind, caring and loving children. I'm so grateful for my emotional, physical and mental health. I thank Allah for giving me inner peace to carry the work I am doing.

Secondly, I would like to thank my children, Hanad, Hibo, Hanan and Harun. My King Hanad, thank you, Hooyo, for stepping up and being a young hardworking man. You encourage me, believe in me, and you always tell me *"You got this, Hooyo."* I am so proud of you and thank you.

My Queen, darling Hibo, Hooyo, I have no words to express my gratitude to you, Hooyo, you are always there to support, help and take care of your younger siblings and you are always checking in with me. I could not do what I do without you, Hooyo macaan. I am grateful to you and thank you, hooyo. I am so proud of you and the beautiful heart you have for your family.

My Princess Hanan, thank you, hooyo, for who you are, you filled my heart with never ending hugs, kisses, love and your personality. You are beautiful inside out. Always be you hooyo. Thank you, hooyo, for always helping and doing your chores.

My prince Harun, hooyo, you are wise beyond your age, you are an old soul. You always worry about me, if I eat, if I sleep, if I am tired, if I have enough money to buy things or go for vacation and it melts my heart knowing how young you are at the age of 9 years old and already worrying things that some grown men don't worry about. You are kind, loving, and always a leader. Thank you, hooyo, for taking care of me and doing your chores at home. I am lucky to call all of you my children, I love, admire, adore, and enjoy being your mom. Thank you all for being everything to me my loves.

Dr. Verna Cornelia Price, I would like to thank you so much for all you do for our girls and leading us women mentors. Your leadership is extremely important, priceless and powerful. I thank you from the bottom of my heart for supporting me and my family when we needed you and always being there for us. We love you and your family.

Mickey Mikeworth, I don't know how to thank you enough. I met you in 2007 and you have been there for me and my family since then. You adapted me, accepted me, believed in me when I did not believe in myself. I am who I am today because of your love, support, encouragement, guidance and with your tough love. You cried with me, laughed with me, drove me to jail, fed me and picked me from the ground when I was at my worst. And Somfam won't be Somfam without you. Thank YOU! You are the older sister I never had, you are my mentor, you are the fun friend, crazy friend and tough friend when I need it. I love you and the world needs more Mickey Mikworth in it.

Pat Aylward. You are a true brother, a brother that I can trust and I can call when I am in need of support, guidance, wisdom and financial help. My children and I are lucky to have you in our lives because we would not have the life we have right now if it wasn't for you. You are our business mentor, support and guide. May Allah guide you, give you a long healthy life, peace and joy. We love you so much and you can always count on us to be there for you when you need us.

Lloyd Brown, thank you for being a brother and a friend to me. Thank you for your support, resources and help to my family, Somfam and all the Somali families that you help and support every single day. Thank you for being my Somali walaalkey.

Marilyn Sharpe, You are the most kind, caring and loving person I know. You have been like a mother to me, you have welcomed me with an open heart and cared for me when I needed to talk. You cooked and fed me. I know I can call you anytime and you will answer my call. You are the mother every girl needs in her life and I wish we had more mothers like you. Thank YOU for being our mom.

Kathryn Shape, Thank you for being a friend and a sister to me and many women. Thank you for the laughter, the stories we share, eating out and being the co-founder of our wonderful women's interfaith group. You are an amazing mom and a mentor to so many Somali youth and your leadership and support for Somfam is unparalleled. I love you and appreciate you.

Molly Jackson, I want to thank you first for being my little sister from another mother. We have been friends first and became sisters through hardships in both our lives. I am proud to call you a sister and an auntie to my children. You have been there for all my family, you were there and helped when I gave birth to Harun, you fed and took care of my children when I was struggling. You took care of Hanan and Harun when I couldn't afford childcare and I had to work. We cooked together, ate, showed movies, cried, laughed, and told crazy stories to each other. We bonded as sisters while we were going through domestic abuse, struggling in life and being single moms. I finished school with your help in the middle of the night while kids were sleeping, but still we had work and life in the morning. You are a true sister and I am honored to call you my sister. Thank you so much for everything you have done for me and my family. We love you my sister.

Bethany Berry, my sister, I would like to thank you for working with me on my memoir, listening to my stories and being patient and flexible with me while juggling a million things. You have been a sister and a friend and thank you for being there for me.

Annette Rondano, I want to thank you for teaching me what kindness is, what giving is and what giving back to someone in need is. Thank you for picking me up from jail and taking me to the nearest restaurant to feed me and my unborn. Thank you for taking my kids places to have fun while I was in jail. Annette, I always remember when I was pregnant with Hanan and I was having false labor. You came to me, you cooked for me and you massage my back and feet to ease the labor pain. You are amazing, gentle, kind, loving and I truly appreciate you so much.

Sheila Dowling, thank you for being a mentor to me. You supported me when I needed help personally and for Somfam and families. I appreciate you and your friendship.

Lastly, I would like to express my deepest appreciation to all my wonderful, supportive, educated, talented, resilient, brave Somali women who are open-minded and understand the meaning of true friendship and sisterhood. The last few years I have met the most amazing Somali women and that truly gave me hope that change is possible inside our community. I love seeing thriving, creative, generous, hardworking and giving sisters. I thank you for all YOU do for our community, family and nation. Know that you are loved, appreciated and needed.

I want to thank the following individuals for their contribution, knowledge, and feedback for the book:

Mickey Mikeworth
Hodan Farah
Jesse Peterson

Dr. Verna Cornelia Price
Dr. Rasheed Farah
Mohamed Hassan (Daryeel)

Resources

Throughout my life, I've listened to motivational speakers that speak to my soul and assist my personal growth and development. Those motivational speakers can range from Islamic scholars that uplift my spirit and strengthen my faith, to self-care, self-love speakers, personal & business growth speakers and many more. Here are several easily searchable speakers that have podcasts or talks you can access for free or very low cost:

Islamic Speakers

These speakers are easily searchable on the internet. They are often featured on podcasts, YouTube, or other platforms.

1. Omar Suleiman
2. Nouman Ali Khan
3. Mufti Menk
4. Belal Assaad
5. Muniba Mazari
6. Dr. Haifaa Younis
7. Hina Khan-Mukhtar
8. Yasmin Mogahe
9. Malala Yousafzai
10. Sheeren Salama

Books

1. **The Power Of People Who Can Change Your Life**, by Dr. Verna Cornelia Price
2. **The Art of Lovingkindness and Peace**, by Jack Kornfield
3. **What to Say When You Talk To Your Self**, by Shad Helmstetter, Ph.D.
4. **The Five Love Languages: The Secret to Love That Lasts,** by Gary Chapman
5. **The Inner Work,** by Mattew Micheletti & Ashley Cottrell
6. **The Mountain Is You,** by Brianna Wiest
7. **Think and Grow Rich,** by Napoleon Hill
8. **Rich Dad Poor Dad,** by Robert Kiyosaki
9. **The Magic of Thinking Big,** by David Schwartz
10. **How To Win Friends & Influence People,** by Dale Carnegie

Other speakers with valuable and motivating messages

1. Tony Robinson
2. Les Brown
3. Wayne Dyer
4. Denzel Washington
5. Oprah Winfrey
6. Robert Kiyosaki
7. Eric Thomas
8. Iyanla Vanzant
9. Deepak Chopra
10. Zig Ziglar

Minority tribes in Somalia

Somalia has many ethnic minority tribes and those include the following and more tribes that are socially, economically, and politically discriminated against.

- Yibir
- Bantu
- Benadiri
- Madhiban
- Musse Deriyo
- Tumal
- Ashraf
- Shekal
- Bajuni
- Rahanweyn
- Howleh
- Yahar
- Hawraarsame

On Tribalism and Discrimination in Somalia

Inspiring Wisdom from Mohamed H. Ali "Daryeel"

Fatoun is my cousin; I met her for the first time in the US during my short visit in 2009. I was there for three months and I came back to Africa after spending a remarkable time in Minnesota. I found Fatoun to be a brave woman struggling alone despite all her challenges in Minnesota

Fatoun struggles in three frontiers as she carries the burden of gender, immigrant and minority. Not only does she struggle in the United States with these three labels, but her struggle was similar back home in Africa.

Gender Equality

Just like many countries in the world, Somalia is a patriarchal society where men control the system of society and government. In such a setting, women are limited from accessing many opportunities to establish themselves, and are exposed to various violations. In the Somali history, one name stands out —a testament to strength, leadership, and cultural significance. Queen Arraweelo, also spelled Arawelo or Caraweelo in Somali. She reflects the essence of resilience in the face of adversity.

The other frontline Fatoun faces is countering effectively discrimination and tribalism. Fatoun and I were born and grew up in Africa inside Somali society. Somalia presents a divisive tribal system that divides communities into"bigger" and "smaller," feeding multiple loyalties that never end from top to the bottom like a peeled onion. Tribalism is one of the oldest primitive social systems in the history of humankind. It maintains fragmented authority in the absence of centralized political institutions.

Tribalism segregates along ethnic lines, dialects, or tribe affiliations. It divides people into "us vs. them" categories - and has contributed to fear and hate. It has negative consequences when it is used to exclude individuals or groups or to take away their rights and status. These negative aspects of tribalism are often fueled by competition and the perception of a common threat. They promote fear, anxiety, and prejudice, all of which make people more susceptible to fake news or distorted information and propaganda about history and heritage, which cause hostility and violence.

Fatoun and I belong to a minority tribe called Yibir scattered among the Somali people inhabited in the Horn of Africa, (Somalia, Djibouti, Ethiopia, and Kenya). My tribe is a victim of tribalism inside Somali society. We are suffering from distorted history, prejudices and biases in information in published colonial history from Somalia. The European scholars obtained distorted information from Somali translators of other tribes who collaborated with scholars which collected and published the opinion of these translators.

To give an example of cultural clash in Somalia, the dominant culture herds camels, has Arabic origins, and is considered to be noble and superior to other cultures. Other nomadic cultures that feature workers in other roles like cowboys, blacksmiths, tailors, fishers, farmers, tanners, artisans, and herbal healers are considered inferior. No intermarriage is allowed between people of the "superior" tribe and the nomadic workers.

Myself, Fatoun and other community members question our tribe history and the root causes of discrimination from other Somalis based on bodily features, skin color, language, and religion. Traditionally Somali people from our Yibir clan associate our community with so many mysteries. Some consider the Yibirs to be associated with Jews, not Somalis, even if we follow the Muslim faith.

The Yibir tribe are said to be the descendants of Mohammad Hanef (king Bu'ur Bayar) who ruled Somaliland before the introduction of Islam. The Yibir tribe is one of the most affected communities in Somalia by tribalism. We have experienced much discrimination.

The Yibir tribe is an indigenous community whose rich heritage is distorted. Religion wise, we are monotheists with a common spiritual heritage that start from Abraham (Hanifa) to Mohamed (Islam). We are linked to three great monotheistic religions—Judaism, Christianity, and Islam. Our descendants of Mohammad to Hanefa are linked to great monotheistic religions -Judaism, Christianity, and Islam. Historically, we are an Indigenous community that has a rich and complex history that spans thousands of years. No deep research is made into our ancient heritage which related to our rule in ancient Somalia, which was called the Macrobia empire and Magan kingdom.

The Magan kingdom existed around 2300 BCE until 550 BCE and established relations with countries bordering the Strait of Hormuz, including the UAE, Oman, Iran and Pakistan. The tallest mount in the UAE is called Yibir Mountain (Jebel Yibir). Similarly, Makraan, which is an amulet that Yibir offers a newborn as a birth certificate in Somalia as part of (Samaanyo) heritage, is called Makran Coast connecting the Strait of Hormuz with the Indian to the Indian Ocean and the Arabian Sea which, is borders Iran and Pakistan on the north, Oman on the south, and the United Arab Emirates on the west.

The Macrobia Empire was a powerful ancient tribal kingdom situated on the Somali peninsula in the Horn of Africa mentioned by Herodotus. It existed during the 1st millennium BCE along the coast of the Atlantic Ocean in the area that is presently Somalia. There are not many written records about these kingdoms. I am highlighting how the tribalism and discrimination affect current generations and their ancient heritage and faith which is part of humanity heritage and ancient culture.

The fight against tribalism in Africa is a new chapter in the larger narrative of humanity's quest for equity and justice. There's still a lot of discrimination against certain tribes and women within Somalia and also within the U.S. Somali communities. The tribal discrimination is devastating and sometimes deadly. It has destroyed many lives. It reminds us that our work is not done until the arbitrary lines of division, whether drawn by race or tribe, are erased and replaced with the unshakable bonds of our shared human experience.

About the Author

Fatoun Ali's mission is to build a better life not just for her own family, but for her entire immigrant community.

In the past 20 years since arriving in the US and losing two children, Fatoun learned English, graduated with a bachelor's degree from university, started her own businesses, and began a non-profit organization that helps Somali youth and families. Now a single mother of four children, Fatoun wears many "hats." She also works in real estate, teaches financial classes, mentors young girls, and writes about her life.

Most importantly, Fatoun builds bridges between Somali culture and American culture. She teaches about Somali history and the difficult refugee experience. She works with schools, social workers, non-profits, and community leaders. Every day, Fatoun tries to help the Somali community in Minnesota be happy, healthy, successful, and safe. She wants Somalis to embrace their culture and thrive in their new American home.

Made in the USA
Middletown, DE
08 February 2025